Joan Didion was born in California and lives in New York City. Her books include *Slouching Towards Bethlehem*, *Miami* and, most recently, *The Year of Magical Thinking*.

Tim Adams is a staff writer at the *Observer*.

Books by JOAN DIDION

SALVADOR

JOAN DIDION

Granta Books
London

Granta Publications, 2/3 Hanover Yard,
Noel Road, London N1 8BE

First published in the US by Simon and Schuster 1983
This edition published by Granta Books 2006

Portions of this book were published in
The New York Review of Books in 1982.

The author wishes to thank the following for their permission to
reprint lines from: The song 'American Pie', written by Don McLean,
published by Mayday Music and Benny Bird Company © 1971. Used
by permission. All rights reserved. The specified abridged excerpt
from pp.63–64 in *The Autumn of the Patriarch* by Gabriel García
Márquez. Translated from the Spanish by Gregory Rabassa.
Copyright © 1975 by Gabriel García Márquez. English translation
copyright © 1976 by Harper & Row, Publishers, Inc. Reprinted by
permission of the publisher. The excerpt from 'Heart of Darkness'
from *Youth* by Joseph Conrad. Reprinted by permission of
Doubleday & Company, Inc. The lines from the poem by Roque
Dalton García from the book *El Salvador: The Face of the
Revolution* by Robert Armstrong and Janet Shenk. Copyright ©
1982, South End Press. Reprinted by permission of the publisher.

A CIP catalogue record for this book is
available from the British Library.

1 3 5 7 9 10 8 6 4 2

ISBN-13: 978-1-86207-868-0
ISBN-10: 1-86207-868-8

Printed and bound in Britain by
Bookmarque Limited, Croydon, Surrey

I am indebted for general background particularly to Thomas P. Anderson's *Matanza: El Salvador's Communist Revolt of 1932* (University of Nebraska Press: Lincoln, 1971) and *The War of the Dispossessed: Honduras and El Salvador, 1969* (University of Nebraska Press: Lincoln, 1981); to David Browning's *El Salvador: Landscape and Society* (Clarendon Press: Oxford, 1971); and to the officers and staff of the United States embassy in San Salvador. I am indebted most of all to my husband, John Gregory Dunne, who was with me in El Salvador and whose notes on, memories about, and interpretations of events there enlarged and informed my own perception of the place.

*This book is for
Robert Silvers
and for
Christopher Dickey*

"All Europe contributed to the making of Kurtz; and by-and-by I learned that, most appropriately, the International Society for the Suppression of Savage Customs had intrusted him with the making of a report, for its future guidance. And he had written it, too. I've seen it. I've read it. It was eloquent, vibrating with eloquence. . . . 'By the simple exercise of our will we can exert a power for good practically unbounded,' etc. etc. From that point he soared and took me with him. The peroration was magnificent, although difficult to remember, you know. It gave me the notion of an exotic Immensity ruled by an august Benevolence. It made me tingle with enthusiasm. This was the unbounded power of eloquence—of words—of burning noble words. There were no practical hints to interrupt the magic current of phrases, unless a kind of note at the foot of the last page, scrawled evidently much later, in an unsteady hand, may be regarded as the exposition of a method. It was very simple, and at the end of that moving appeal to every altruistic sentiment it blazed at you, luminous and terrifying, like a flash of lightning in a serene sky: 'Exterminate all the brutes!'"

—Joseph Conrad,
Heart of Darkness

INTRODUCTION

The greatest reporters always make the world outside their head sound like the one inside it. Joan Didion's places and her people are uniformly Didion-esque, in the way that Hemingway's wars appeared made for his typewriter, and Orwell's world always marshalled itself into something recognizably Orwellian. This is not a reductive point; it does not mean that such writers distort what is out there to fit their preconceptions. It is rather that their vision is so true, and their voice so attuned to a moment that it can accommodate and interrogate anything real life can throw up.

The only time I met Joan Didion, at her apartment off Park Avenue, I watched this phenomenon at work. Breaking the first rule of all journalists – never interview other journalists – I had gone to see her armed with a tape recorder, hoping to get her talking about the ways in which she had made herself so alive to her times, the manner in which she had brought her distinctive nervous energy to bear on the world.

Instead of talking much, she simply gave a demonstration of that restless angst. Her husband John Gregory Dunne was on a flight that had been rerouted because of snow and she had no idea where he was headed, so she fretted for his safe landing, and spent nearly all of our allotted couple of hours making tortuous, hesitant calls to airline officials and remote airports trying to track him down. She made precise notes, got passed from one desk to the next, waited fidgeting by the phone. I had the sense that all of her days, whether off duty or on, passed like this; that there was always something urgent and troubling to discover, and an interminable love–hate relationship with the processes of finding out. In this sense, awfully, Didion's *The Year of Magical Thinking* – her recent account of the deaths of both her husband and her daughter – felt a lot like a book she had been learning all of her life to write, one in which all of her worst fears came true.

Back in the 1970s, Didion was grouped with Tom Wolfe's new journalists because she never allowed you to forget that it was her doing the looking, her doing the note-taking and her doing the writing. Really, though, she has always been a one-off, in that her presence in her journalism has rarely seemed to be about ego, rather about compulsion.

From the outset, she liked to characterize herself as a reluctant understander of the world, someone who felt fated to know things but who was made almost physically ill by the repercussions of knowledge. Her introduction to her first collection of writing *Slouching Towards Bethlehem*, sets out a personal manifesto for her neurotic realism; 'I am bad at interviewing people . . .' she wrote. 'I do not like to make telephone calls, and would not like to count the mornings I have sat on some Best Western motel bed somewhere and tried to force myself to put through the call to the district attorney. My only advantage as a reporter is that I am so physically small, so temperamentally unobtrusive, and so neurotically inarticulate that people tend to forget that my presence runs counter to their best interests . . .'

It is an overlooked fact – particularly in Hollywood representations of reporters – that the best print journalists are often cripplingly awkward in the world. Their writing allows them a fluency that they have always craved. The adjective that most readily attaches itself to Didion is 'bird-like', which not only describes her physical presence, but also her twitchy, dislocated appreciation of information, and her sense of present danger. *Salvador*, of all her books, provides the truest expression of this quality. No situation she had been in before matched her sense of the paranoia and vacancy at the heart of wider American 'progress' so exactly. In San Salvador in 1982 there was no fixed vantage even for her impressions. Facts, in a country where the numbers of the dead shifted according to your point of view, were impossible to come by.

That did not stop her letting you watch her try to pile them up, however. In the opening to her novel *The Last Thing He Wanted* Didion wrote, typically, 'Some real things have happened lately' and it is the search for those kinds of things, among layers of rumour and propaganda, that keep her going in *Salvador*. She finds some of them at the morgue, or between the lines of newspapers, or in the televised interviews of the hopes and dreams of beauty queens. She gravitates inevitably to the places where she always gets her bearings: to the city's airport and shopping malls.

In *The White Album* she wrote of 'taking, by correspondence, a University of California Extension course in Shopping Center theory' and of her fantasies of running shopping malls herself. 'I wanted to build them because I had fallen into the habit of writing fiction, and I had it in my head that a couple of good centers might support this habit . . .' Though her studies came to nothing they came in handy in El Salvador. No one else, for example, could show you fear in a playlist of piped music: 'One afternoon when I had run out of the Halazone tablets I dropped every night into the pitcher of tap water (a demented *gringa* gesture, I knew even then, in a country where everyone not born there was at least mildly ill, including the nurse at the American embassy), I walked across the street from the Camino Real to the Metrocenter, which is refered to locally as "Central America's largest shopping mall". I found no Halazone at the Metrocenter but became absorbed in making notes about the mall itself, about the Muzak playing "I Left My Heart in San Francisco" and "American Pie" (*"singing this will be the day that I die . . ."*) . . .'

Didion was only in El Salvador for a fortnight or so to do her looking, working on assignment for the *New York Review of Books*, though she makes it feel like a lifetime of attention. She carried with her in those two weeks all of her connoisseur's appreciation of the workings of power, and the banalities of terror. Reviewing this book in the *Sunday Times* Paul Theroux remarked that it was a good book about 'being nervous' but not a great book about El Salvador. Theroux, perhaps deliberately, missed Didion's point: that nervousness was exactly where El Salvador began and ended, that nervousness, and surprise, and routine horror were always what state terror demanded and demonstrated.

As a primer in the repetitive self-delusions of American foreign policy, *Salvador* could hardly be bettered. Reaganite placemen, propping up murderous anti-communist regimes, could look at themselves in the mirror and convince the face there that it was engaged in encouraging 'nascent democratic institutions'. Everything, even daily mass-murder, torture and disappearance, was to be taken as evidence of the steady advance of freedom, and the pursuit of justice. Didion's account of her lunch with the ambassador Deane Hinton says much about the failure of American intervention in any number of wars and conflicts up to the present day. 'The American effort in El Salvador seemed based on a kind of auto-suggestion, a dreamwork devised to obscure any intelligence that might trouble the dreamer,' she noted. 'At a point between the salad and the profiteroles, it occurred to me that we were talking exclusively about the appearances of things, about how the situation might be made to look better, about trying to get the Salvadoran government to "appear" to do what the American government needed done in order to make it "appear" that American aid was justified.'

In skewering this gap between appearance and reality Didion needed all of her range of tone and nuance. No journalist has quite her grasp of the ways in and out of irony but this is the book where she first discovered that the cool cynicism she had learned in California, which could quite perfectly illuminate the morality of 'some dreamers after the golden dream' or the slow death of Hollywood, might not always be fully adequate to the task at hand. Ennui and alienation give way occasionally in *Salvador* to a sort of helplessness of looking, which for Didion is something like outrage. 'As I waited to cross back over the Boulevard de los Heroes to the Camino Real I noticed soldiers herding a young civilian into a van, their guns at the boy's back, and I walked straight ahead, not wanting to see anything at all.'

In this admission of the limits of curiosity Didion in Salvador turns the most basic journalistic principle – that the truth is out there – on its head. Of her courageous trip out to Gotera, the 'mean hill country' where some of the worst atrocities of the government's terror campaign against its own people had taken place she concludes simply that 'nothing came of the day but overheard rumors, indefinite observations, fragments of information that might or might not fit into a pattern we did not perceive'. Few reporters are so keen to admit to the partiality of their understanding as Didion, but her writing exactly demonstrates the role of the journalist in a world where information is everywhere and truth is nowhere to find.

In place of certainty, or often even of opinion, she tirelessly dramatizes her particular sifting of scraps and clues, the importance of the effort of trying to bear witness, and places her faith in the idea that it might be enough. Georgia O'Keeffe has long been her heroine. Didion always liked, as she once wrote in an essay on O'Keeffe, the idea that 'style is character'. that 'every choice made alone – every word chosen or rejected, every brushstroke laid or not laid down – betrayed one's character'. It is the test of a style, particularly one as complex and engaging as Didion's, that it can contain all that it needs to without appearing mannered. *Salvador* is the book where she most tellingly puts that style, that character, to the test of the worst of the world. It is not found wanting.

Tim Adams

SALVADOR

THE three-year-old El Salvador International Airport is glassy and white and splendidly isolated, conceived during the waning of the Molina "National Transformation" as convenient less to the capital (San Salvador is forty miles away, until recently a drive of several hours) than to a central hallucination of the Molina and Romero regimes, the projected beach resorts, the Hyatt, the Pacific Paradise, tennis, golf, water-skiing, condos, *Costa del Sol*; the visionary invention of a tourist industry in yet another republic where the leading natural cause of death is gastrointestinal infection. In the general absence of tourists these hotels have since been abandoned, ghost resorts on the empty Pacific beaches, and to land at this airport built to service them is to plunge directly into a state in which no ground is solid, no depth of field reliable, no perception so definite that it might not dissolve into its reverse.

The only logic is that of acquiescence. Immigration is negotiated in a thicket of automatic weapons, but by whose authority the weapons are brandished (Army or National Guard or National Police or Customs Police or Treasury Police or one of a continuing proliferation of other shadowy and overlapping forces) is a blurred point. Eye contact is avoided. Documents are scrutinized upside down. Once clear of the airport, on the new highway that slices through green hills rendered phosphorescent by the cloud cover of the tropical rainy season, one sees mainly underfed cattle and mongrel dogs and armored vehicles, vans and trucks and Cherokee Chiefs fitted with reinforced steel and bulletproof Plexiglas an inch thick. Such vehicles are a fixed feature of local life, and are popularly associated with disappearance and death. There was the Cherokee Chief seen following the Dutch television crew killed in Chalatenango province in March of 1982. There was the red Toyota three-quarter-ton pickup sighted near the van driven by the four American Catholic workers on the night they were killed in 1980. There were, in the late spring and summer of 1982, the three Toyota panel trucks, one yellow, one blue, and one green, none bearing plates, reported present at each of the mass detentions (a "detention" is another fixed feature of local life, and often precedes a "disappearance") in the Amatepec district of San Salvador. These are the details—the models and colors of armored vehicles, the makes and calibers of weapons, the particular methods of dismemberment and decapitation used in particular instances—on which the visitor to Salvador learns immediately to concentrate, to the exclusion of past or future concerns, as in a prolonged amnesiac fugue.

Terror is the given of the place. Black-and-white police cars cruise in pairs, each with the barrel of a rifle

extruding from an open window. Roadblocks materialize at random, soldiers fanning out from trucks and
taking positions, fingers always on triggers, safeties
clicking on and off. Aim is taken as if to pass the time.
Every morning *El Diario de Hoy* and *La Prensa
Gráfica* carry cautionary stories. *"Una madre y sus
dos hijos fueron asesinados con arma cortante (corvo)
por ocho sujetos desconocidos el lunes en la noche"*:
A mother and her two sons hacked to death in their
beds by eight *desconocidos*, unknown men. The same
morning's paper: the unidentified body of a young
man, strangled, found on the shoulder of a road. Same
morning, different story: the unidentified bodies of
three young men, found on another road, their faces
partially destroyed by bayonets, one faced carved to
represent a cross.

It is largely from these reports in the newspapers that
the United States embassy compiles its body counts,
which are transmitted to Washington in a weekly dis-
patch referred to by embassy people as "the grim-
gram." These counts are presented in a kind of tortured
code that fails to obscure what is taken for granted in
El Salvador, that government forces do most of the
killing. In a January 15 1982 memo to Washington,
for example, the embassy issued a "guarded" break-
down on its count of 6,909 "reported" political murders between September 16 1980 and September 15
1981. Of these 6,909, according to the memo, 922 were
"believed committed by security forces," 952 "believed committed by leftist terrorists," 136 "believed
committed by rightist terrorists," and 4,889 "com-

mitted by unknown assailants," the famous *desconocidos* favored by those San Salvador newspapers still publishing. (The figures actually add up not to 6,909 but to 6,899, leaving ten in a kind of official limbo.) The memo continued:

> "The uncertainty involved here can be seen in the fact that responsibility cannot be fixed in the majority of cases. We note, however, that it is generally believed in El Salvador that a large number of the unexplained killings are carried out by the security forces, officially or unofficially. The Embassy is aware of dramatic claims that have been made by one interest group or another in which the security forces figure as the primary agents of murder here. El Salvador's tangled web of attack and vengeance, traditional criminal violence and political mayhem make this an impossible charge to sustain. In saying this, however, we make no attempt to lighten the responsibility for the deaths of many hundreds, and perhaps thousands, which can be attributed to the security forces. . . ."

The body count kept by what is generally referred to in San Salvador as "the Human Rights Commission" is higher than the embassy's, and documented periodically by a photographer who goes out looking for bodies. These bodies he photographs are often broken into unnatural positions, and the faces to which the bodies are attached (when they are attached) are equally unnatural, sometimes unrecognizable as human faces, obliterated by acid or beaten to a mash of misplaced ears and teeth or slashed ear to ear and invaded by insects. *"Encontrado en Antiguo Cuscatlán el día 25 de Marzo 1982: camison de dormir celeste,"* the typed caption reads on one photograph: found in Antiguo Cuscatlán March 25 1982 wearing a sky-blue nightshirt. The captions are laconic. Found in Soyapango May 21 1982. Found in Mejicanos June 11 1982. Found at El Playón May 30 1982, white shirt, purple pants, black shoes.

The photograph accompanying that last caption shows a body with no eyes, because the vultures got to it before the photographer did. There is a special kind of practical information that the visitor to El Salvador acquires immediately, the way visitors to other places acquire information about the currency rates, the hours for the museums. In El Salvador one learns that vultures go first for the soft tissue, for the eyes, the exposed genitalia, the open mouth. One learns that an open mouth can be used to make a specific point, can be stuffed with something emblematic; stuffed, say, with a penis, or, if the point has to do with land title, stuffed with some of the dirt in question. One learns that hair deteriorates less rapidly than flesh, and that a skull surrounded by a perfect corona of hair is a not uncommon sight in the body dumps.

All forensic photographs induce in the viewer a certain protective numbness, but dissociation is more difficult here. In the first place these are not, technically, "forensic" photographs, since the evidence they document will never be presented in a court of law. In the second place the disfigurement is too routine. The locations are too near, the dates too recent. There is the presence of the relatives of the disappeared: the women who sit every day in this cramped office on the grounds of the archdiocese, waiting to look at the spiral-bound photo albums in which the photographs are kept. These albums have plastic covers bearing soft-focus color photographs of young Americans in dating situations (strolling through autumn foliage on one album, recumbent in a field of daisies on another), and the women, looking for the bodies of their husbands and brothers and sisters and children, pass them from hand to hand without comment or expression.

> "One of the more shadowy elements of the violent scene here [is] the death squad. Existence of these groups has long been disputed, but not by many Salvadorans. . . . Who constitutes the death squads is yet another difficult question. We do not believe that these squads exist as permanent formations but rather as ad hoc vigilante groups that coalesce according to perceived need. Membership is also uncertain, but in addition to civilians we believe that both on- and off-duty members of the security forces are participants. This was unofficially confirmed by right-wing spokesman Maj. Roberto D'Aubuisson who stated in an interview in early 1981 that security force members utilize the guise of the death squad when a potentially embarrassing or odious task needs to be performed."

> —*From the confidential but later declassified January 15, 1982 memo previously cited, drafted for the State Department by the political section at the embassy in San Salvador.*

The dead and pieces of the dead turn up in El Salvador everywhere, every day, as taken for granted as in a nightmare, or a horror movie. Vultures of course suggest the presence of a body. A knot of children on the street suggests the presence of a body. Bodies turn up in the brush of vacant lots, in the garbage thrown down ravines in the richest districts, in public rest rooms, in bus stations. Some are dropped in Lake Ilopango, a few miles east of the city, and wash up near the lakeside cottages and clubs frequented by what remains in San Salvador of the sporting bourgeoisie. Some still turn up at El Playón, the lunar lava field of rotting human flesh visible at one time or another on every television screen in America but characterized in June of 1982 in the *El Salvador News Gazette*, an English-language weekly edited by an American named Mario Rosenthal, as an "uncorroborated story . . . dredged up from the files of leftist propaganda." Others turn up at Puerta del Diablo, above Parque Balboa, a national *Turicentro* described as recently as the April–July 1982 issue of *Aboard TACA*, the magazine provided passengers on the national airline of El Salvador, as "offering excellent subjects for color photography."

I drove up to Puerta del Diablo one morning in June of 1982, past the Casa Presidencial and the camouflaged watch towers and heavy concentrations of troops and arms south of town, on up a narrow road narrowed further by landslides and deep crevices in the roadbed, a drive so insistently premonitory that after a while I began to hope that I would pass Puerta del Diablo without knowing it, just miss it, write it off, turn around and go back. There was however no way of missing it. Puerta del Diablo is a "view site" in an older and distinctly literary tradition, nature as lesson, an immense cleft rock through which half of El Salvador seems framed, a site so romantic and "mystical," so theatrically sacrificial in aspect, that it might be a cosmic parody of nineteenth-century landscape painting. The place presents itself as pathetic fallacy: the sky "broods," the stones "weep," a constant seepage of water weighting the ferns and moss. The foliage is thick and slick with moisture. The only sound is a steady buzz, I believe of cicadas.

Body dumps are seen in El Salvador as a kind of visitors' must-do, difficult but worth the detour. "Of course you have seen El Playón," an aide to President Alvaro Magaña said to me one day, and proceeded to discuss the site geologically, as evidence of the country's geothermal resources. He made no mention of the bodies. I was unsure if he was sounding me out or simply found the geothermal aspect of overriding interest. One difference between El Playón and Puerta del Diablo is that most bodies at El Playón appear to have been killed somewhere else, and then dumped; at Puerta del Diablo the executions are believed to occur in place, at the top, and the bodies thrown over. Sometimes reporters will speak of wanting to spend the night at Puerta del Diablo, in order to document the actual execution, but at the time I was in Salvador no one had.

The aftermath, the daylight aspect, is well documented. "Nothing fresh today, I hear," an embassy officer said when I mentioned that I had visited Puerta del Diablo. "Were there any on top?" someone else asked. "There were supposed to have been three on top yesterday." The point about whether or not there had been any on top was that usually it was necessary to go down to see bodies. The way down is hard. Slabs of stone, slippery with moss, are set into the vertiginous cliff, and it is down this cliff that one begins the descent to the bodies, or what is left of the bodies, pecked and maggoty masses of flesh, bone, hair. On some days there have been helicopters circling, tracking those making the descent. Other days there have been militia at the top, in the clearing where the road seems to run out, but on the morning I was there the only people on top were a man and a woman and three small children, who played in the wet grass while the woman started and stopped a Toyota pickup. She appeared to be learning how to drive. She drove forward and then back toward the edge, apparently following the man's signals, over and over again.

We did not speak, and it was only later, down the mountain and back in the land of the provisionally living, that it occurred to me that there was a definite question about why a man and a woman might choose a well-known body dump for a driving lesson. This was one of a number of occasions, during the two weeks my husband and I spent in El Salvador, on which I came to understand, in a way I had not understood before, the exact mechanism of terror.

Whenever I had nothing better to do in San Salvador I would walk up in the leafy stillness of the San Benito and Escalón districts, where the hush at midday is broken only by the occasional crackle of a walkie-talkie, the click of metal moving on a weapon. I recall a day in San Benito when I opened my bag to check an address, and heard the clicking of metal on metal all up and down the street. On the whole no one walks up here, and pools of blossoms lie undisturbed on the sidewalks. Most of the houses in San Benito are more recent than those in Escalón, less idiosyncratic and probably smarter, but the most striking architectural features in both districts are not the houses but their walls, walls built upon walls, walls stripped of the usual copa de oro and bougainvillea, walls that reflect successive generations of violence: the original stone, the additional five or six or ten feet of brick, and finally the barbed wire, sometimes concertina, sometimes electrified; walls with watch towers, gun ports, closed-circuit television cameras, walls now reaching twenty and thirty feet.

San Benito and Escalón appear on the embassy security maps as districts of relatively few "incidents," but they remain districts in which a certain oppressive uneasiness prevails. In the first place there are always "incidents"—detentions and deaths and disappearances—in the *barrancas*, the ravines lined with shanties that fall down behind the houses with the walls and the guards and the walkie-talkies; one day in Escalón I was introduced to a woman who kept the lean-to that served as a grocery in a *barranca* just above the Hotel Sheraton. She was sticking prices on bars of Camay and Johnson's baby soap, stopping occasionally to sell a plastic bag or two filled with crushed ice and Coca-

Cola, and all the while she talked in a low voice about her fear, about her eighteen-year-old son, about the boys who had been taken out and shot on successive nights recently in a neighboring *barranca*.

In the second place there is, in Escalón, the presence of the Sheraton itself, a hotel that has figured rather too prominently in certain local stories involving the disappearance and death of Americans. The Sheraton always seems brighter and more mildly festive than either the Camino Real or the Presidente, with children in the pool and flowers and pretty women in pastel dresses, but there are usually several bulletproofed Cherokee Chiefs in the parking area, and the men drinking in the lobby often carry the little zippered purses that in San Salvador suggest not passports or credit cards but Browning 9-mm. pistols.

It was at the Sheraton that one of the few American *desaparecidos*, a young free-lance writer named John Sullivan, was last seen, in December of 1980. It was also at the Sheraton, after eleven on the evening of January 3 1981, that the two American advisers on agrarian reform, Michael Hammer and Mark Pearlman, were killed, along with the Salvadoran director of the Institute for Agrarian Transformation, José Rodolfo Viera. The three were drinking coffee in a dining room off the lobby, and whoever killed them used an Ingram MAC-10, without sound suppressor, and then walked out through the lobby, unapprehended. The Sheraton has even turned up in the investigation into the December 1980 deaths of the four American churchwomen, Sisters Ita Ford and Maura Clarke, the two Maryknoll

23

nuns; Sister Dorothy Kazel, the Ursuline nun; and Jean Donovan, the lay volunteer. In *Justice in El Salvador: A Case Study*, prepared and released in July of 1982 in New York by the Lawyers' Committee for International Human Rights, there appears this note:

> "On December 19, 1980, the [Duarte government's] Special Investigative Commission reported that 'a red Toyota ¾-ton pickup was seen leaving (the crime scene) at about 11:00 P.M. on December 2' and that 'a red splotch on the burned van' of the churchwomen was being checked to determine whether the paint splotch 'could be the result of a collision between that van and the red Toyota pickup.' By February 1981, the Maryknoll Sisters' Office of Social Concerns, which has been actively monitoring the investigation, received word from a source which it considered reliable that the FBI had matched the red splotch on the burned van with a red Toyota pickup belonging to the Sheraton hotel in San Salvador. . . . Subsequent to the FBI's alleged matching of the paint splotch and a Sheraton truck, the State Department has claimed, in a communication with the families of the churchwomen, that 'the FBI could not determine the source of the paint scraping.'"

There is also mention in this study of a young Salvadoran businessman named Hans Christ (his father was a German who arrived in El Salvador at the end of World War II), a part owner of the Sheraton. Hans Christ lives now in Miami, and that his name should have even come up in the Maryknoll investigation made many people uncomfortable, because it was Hans Christ, along with his brother-in-law, Ricardo Sol Meza, who, in April of 1981, was first charged with the murders of Michael Hammer and Mark Pearlman and José Rodolfo Viera at the Sheraton. These charges were later dropped, and were followed by a series of other charges, arrests, releases, expressions of "dismay" and "incredulity" from the American embassy, and even, in the fall of 1982, confessions to the killings from two former National Guard corporals, who testified that Hans Christ had led them through the lobby and pointed out the victims. Hans Christ and Ricardo Sol Meza have said that the dropped case against them was a government frame-up, and that they were only having drinks at the Sheraton the night of the killings, with a National Guard intelligence officer. It was logical for Hans Christ and Ricardo Sol Meza to have drinks at the Sheraton because they both had interests in the hotel, and Ricardo Sol Meza had just opened a roller disco, since closed, off the lobby into which the killers walked that night. The killers were described by witnesses as well dressed, their faces covered. The room from which they walked was at the time I was in San Salvador no longer a restaurant, but the marks left by the bullets were still visible, on the wall facing the door.

Whenever I had occasion to visit the Sheraton I was apprehensive, and this apprehension came to color the entire Escalón district for me, even its lower reaches, where there were people and movies and restaurants. I recall being struck by it on the canopied porch of a restaurant near the Mexican embassy, on an evening when rain or sabotage or habit had blacked out the city and I became abruptly aware, in the light cast by a passing car, of two human shadows, silhouettes illuminated by the headlights and then invisible again. One shadow sat behind the smoked glass windows of a Cherokee Chief parked at the curb in front of the restaurant; the other crouched between the pumps at the Esso station next door, carrying a rifle. It seemed to me unencouraging that my husband and I were the only people seated on the porch. In the absence of the headlights the candle on our table provided the only light, and I fought the impulse to blow it out. We continued talking, carefully. Nothing came of this, but I did not forget the sensation of having been in a single instant demoralized, undone, humiliated by fear, which is what I meant when I said that I came to understand in El Salvador the mechanism of terror.

"3/3/81: Roberto D'Aubuisson, a former Salvadoran army intelligence officer, holds a press conference and says that before the U.S. presidential election he had been in touch with a number of Reagan advisers and those contacts have continued. The armed forces should ask the junta to resign, D'Aubuisson says. He refuses to name a date for the action, but says 'March is, I think, a very interesting month.' He also calls for the abandonment of the economic reforms. D'Aubuisson had been accused of plotting to overthrow the government on two previous occasions. Observers speculate that since D'Aubuisson is able to hold the news conference and pass freely between Salvador and Guatemala, he must enjoy considerable support among some sections of the army. . . . 3/4/81: In San Salvador, the U.S. embassy is fired upon; no one is injured. Chargé d'Affaires Frederic Chapin says, 'This incident has all the hallmarks of a D'Aubuisson operation. Let me state to you that we oppose coups and we have no intention of being intimidated.'"

—*From the "Chronology of Events Related to Salvadoran Situation" prepared periodically by the United States embassy in San Salvador.*

"Since the Exodus from Egypt, historians have written of those who sacrificed and struggled for freedom: the stand at Thermopylae, the revolt of Spartacus, the storming of the Bastille, the Warsaw uprising in World War II. More recently we have seen evidence of this same human impulse in one of the developing nations in Central America. For months and months the world news media covered the fighting in El Salvador. Day after day, we were treated to stories and film slanted toward the brave freedom fighters battling oppressive government forces in behalf of the silent, suffering people of that tortured country. Then one day those silent suffering people were offered a chance to vote to choose the kind of government they wanted. Suddenly the freedom fighters in the hills were exposed for what they really are: Cuban-backed guerrillas. . . . On election day the people of El Salvador, an unprecedented [1.5 million] of them, braved ambush and gunfire, trudging miles to vote for freedom."

—*President Reagan, in his June 8 1982 speech before both houses of the British Parliament, referring to the March 28 1982 election which resulted in the ascension of Roberto D'Aubuisson to the presidency of the Constituent Assembly.*

From whence he shall come to judge the quick and the dead. I happened to read President Reagan's speech one evening in San Salvador when President Reagan was in fact on television, with Doris Day, in *The Winning Team*, a 1952 Warner Brothers picture about the baseball pitcher Grover Cleveland Alexander. I reached the stand at Thermopylae at about the time that *el salvador del Salvador* began stringing cranberries and singing "Old St. Nicholas" with Miss Day. "*Muy bonita*," he said when she tried out a rocking chair in her wedding dress. "*Feliz Navidad*," they cried, and, in accented English, "*Play ball!*"

As it happened "play ball" was a phrase I had come to associate in El Salvador with Roberto D'Aubuisson and his followers in the Nationalist Republican Alliance, or ARENA. "It's a process of letting certain people know they're going to have to play ball," embassy people would say, and: "You take a guy who's young, and everything 'young' implies, you send him signals, he plays ball, then we play ball." American diction in this situation tends toward the studied casual, the can-do, as if sheer cool and Bailey bridges could shape the place up. Elliott Abrams told *The New York Times* in July of 1982 that punishment within the Salvadoran military could be "a very important sign that you can't do this stuff any more," meaning kill the citizens. "If you clean up your act, all things are possible," is the way Jeremiah O'Leary, a special assistant to U.S. national security adviser William Clark, described the American diplomatic effort in an interview given *The Los Angeles Times* just after the March 28 1982 election. He was speculating on how Ambassador Deane Hinton might be dealing with D'Aubuisson. "I kind of picture him saying, 'Goddamnit, Bobbie, you've got a problem and . . . if you're what everyone said you are, you're going to make it hard for everybody.'"

Roberto D'Aubuisson is a chain smoker, as were many of the people I met in El Salvador, perhaps because it is a country in which the possibility of achieving a death related to smoking remains remote. I never met Major D'Aubuisson, but I was always interested in the adjectives used to describe him. "Pathological" was the adjective, modifying "killer," used by former ambassador Robert E. White (it was White who refused D'Aubuisson a visa, after which, according to the embassy's "Chronology of Events" for June 30 1980, "D'Aubuisson manages to enter the U.S. illegally and spends two days in Washington holding press conferences and attending luncheons before turning himself in to immigration authorities"), but "pathological" is not a word one heard in-country, where meaning tends to be transmitted in code.

In-country one heard "young" (the "and everything 'young' implies" part was usually left tacit), even immature"; "impetuous," "impulsive," "impatient," "nervous," "volatile," "high-strung," "kind of coiled-up," and, most frequently, "intense," or just "tense." Offhand it struck me that Roberto D'Aubuisson had some reason to be tense, in that General José Guillermo García, who had remained a main player through several changes of government, might logically perceive him as the wild card who could queer everybody's ability to refer to his election as a vote for freedom. As I write this I realize that I have fallen into the Salvadoran mindset, which turns on plot, and, since half the players at any given point in the game are in exile, on the phrase "in touch with."

"I've known D'Aubuisson a long time," I was told by Alvaro Magaña, the banker the Army made, over D'Aubuisson's rather frenzied objections ("We stopped that one on the one-yard line," Deane Hinton told me about D'Aubuisson's play to block Magaña), provisional president of El Salvador. We were sitting in his office upstairs at the Casa Presidencial, an airy and spacious building in the tropical colonial style, and he was drinking cup after Limoges cup of black coffee, smoking one cigarette with each, carefully, an unwilling actor who intended to survive the accident of being cast in this production. "Since Molina was president. I used to come here to see Molina, D'Aubuisson would be here, he was a young man in military intelligence, I'd see him here." He gazed toward the corridor that opened onto the interior courtyard, with cannas, oleander, a fountain not in operation. "When we're alone now I try to talk to him. I do talk to him, he's coming for lunch today. He never calls me Alvaro, it's always *usted, Señor, Doctor*. I call him Roberto. I say, Roberto, don't do this, don't do that, you know."

Magaña studied in the United States, at Chicago, and his four oldest children are now in the United States, one son at Vanderbilt, a son and a daughter at Santa Clara, and another daughter near Santa Clara, at Notre Dame in Belmont. He is connected by money, education, and temperament to oligarchal families. All the players here are densely connected: Magaña's sister, who lives in California, is the best friend of Nora Ungo,

the wife of Guillermo Ungo, and Ungo spoke to
Magaña's sister in August of 1982 when he was in
California raising money for the FMLN–FDR, which
is what the opposition to the Salvadoran government
was called this year. The membership and even the
initials of this opposition tend to the fluid, but the
broad strokes are these: the FMLN–FDR is the coalition between the Revolutionary Democratic Front
(FDR) and the five guerrilla groups joined together in
the Farabundo Martí National Liberation Front
(FMLN). These five groups are the Salvadoran Communist Party (PCS), the Popular Forces of Liberation
(FPL), the Revolutionary Party of Central American
Workers (PRTC), the People's Revolutionary Army
(ERP), and the Armed Forces of National Resistance
(FARN). Within each of these groups, there are fur-
ther factions, and sometimes even further initials, as in
the PRS and LP-28 of the ERP.

During the time that D'Aubuisson was trying to stop
Magaña's appointment as provisional president, members of ARENA, which is supported heavily by other
oligarchal elements, passed out leaflets referring to
Magaña, predictably, as a communist, and, more in-
terestingly, as "the little Jew." The manipulation of
anti-Semitism is an undercurrent in Salvadoran life that
is not much discussed and probably worth some study,
since it refers to a tension within the oligarchy itself,
the tension between those families who solidified their
holdings in the mid-nineteenth century and those later
families, some of them Jewish, who arrived in El Salvador and entrenched themselves around 1900. I recall
asking a well-off Salvadoran about the numbers of his

acquaintances within the oligarchy who have removed themselves and their money to Miami. "Mostly the Jews," he said.

> "In San Salvador
> in the year 1965
> the best sellers
> of the three most important
> book stores
> were:
> The Protocols of the Elders of Zion;
> a few books by
> diarrhetic Somerset Maugham;
> a book of disagreeably
> obvious poems
> by a lady with a European name
> who nonetheless writes in Spanish about our
> country
> and a collection of
> Reader's Digest condensed novels."

—*"San Salvador" by Roque Dalton, translated by Edward Baker.*

The late Roque Dalton García was born into the Salvadoran bourgeoisie in 1935, spent some years in Havana, came home in 1973 to join the ERP, or the People's Revolutionary Army, and, in 1975, was executed, on charges that he was a CIA agent, by his own comrades. The actual executioner was said to be Joaquín Villalobos, who is now about thirty years old, commander of the ERP, and a key figure in the FMLN, which, as the Mexican writer Gabriel Zaid pointed out in the winter 1982 issue of *Dissent,* has as one of its support groups the Roque Dalton Cultural Brigade. The Dalton execution is frequently cited by people who want to stress that "the other side kills people too, you know," an argument common mainly among those, like the State Department, with a stake in whatever government is current in El Salvador, since, if it is taken for granted in Salvador that the government kills, it is also taken for granted that the other side kills; that everyone has killed, everyone kills now, and, if the history of the place suggests any pattern, everyone will continue to kill.

"Don't say I said this, but there are no issues here," I was told by a high-placed Salvadoran. "There are only ambitions." He meant of course not that there were no ideas in conflict but that the conflicting ideas were held exclusively by people he knew, that, whatever the outcome of any fighting or negotiation or coup or countercoup, the Casa Presidencial would ultimately be occupied not by *campesinos* and Maryknolls but by the already entitled, by a Guillermo Ungo or a Joaquín Villalobos or even by Roque Dalton's son, Juan José Dalton, or by Juan José Dalton's comrade in the FPL, José Antonio Morales Carbonell, the guerrilla son of José Antonio Morales Ehrlich, a former member of the Duarte junta who had himself been in exile during the Romero regime. In an open letter written shortly before his arrest in San Salvador in June 1980, José Antonio Morales Carbonell had charged his father with an insufficient appreciation of "Yankee imperialism." José Antonio Morales Carbonell and Juan José Dalton tried together to enter the United States in the summer of 1982, for a speaking engagement in San Francisco, but were refused visas by the American embassy in Mexico City.

Whatever the issues were that had divided Morales Carbonell and his father and Roque Dalton and Joaquín Villalobos, the prominent Salvadoran to whom I was talking seemed to be saying, they were issues that fell somewhere outside the lines normally drawn to indicate "left" and "right." That this man saw *la situación* as only one more realignment of power among the entitled, a conflict of "ambitions" rather than "issues," was, I recognized, what many people would call a conventional bourgeois view of civil conflict, and offered no solutions, but the people with solutions to offer were mainly somewhere else, in Mexico or Panama or Washington.

The place brings everything into question. One afternoon when I had run out of the Halazone tablets I dropped every night in a pitcher of tap water (a demented *gringa* gesture, I knew even then, in a country where everyone not born there was at least mildly ill, including the nurse at the American embassy), I walked across the street from the Camino Real to the Metrocenter, which is referred to locally as "Central America's Largest Shopping Mall." I found no Halazone at the Metrocenter but became absorbed in making notes about the mall itself, about the Muzak playing "I Left My Heart in San Francisco" and "American

Pie" ("... *singing this will be the day that I die ...*")
although the record store featured a cassette called
Classics of Paraguay, about the *pâté de foie gras* for
sale in the supermarket, about the guard who did the
weapons check on everyone who entered the supermarket, about the young matrons in tight Sergio Va-
lente jeans, trailing maids and babies behind them and
buying towels, big beach towels printed with maps of
Manhattan that featured Bloomingdale's; about the
number of things for sale that seemed to suggest a
fashion for "smart drinking," to evoke modish cock-
tail hours. There were bottles of Stolichnaya vodka
packaged with glasses and mixer, there were ice buck-
ets, there were bar carts of every conceivable design,
displayed with sample bottles.

This was a shopping center that embodied the future
for which El Salvador was presumably being saved,
and I wrote it down dutifully, this being the kind of
"color" I knew how to interpret, the kind of inductive
irony, the detail that was supposed to illuminate the
story. As I wrote it down I realized that I was no longer
much interested in this kind of irony, that this was a
story that would not be illuminated by such details,
that this was a story that would perhaps not be illuminated at all, that this was perhaps even less a "story"
than a true *noche obscura.* As I waited to cross back
over the Boulevard de los Heroes to the Camino Real
I noticed soldiers herding a young civilian into a van,
their guns at the boy's back, and I walked straight
ahead, not wanting to see anything at all.

"12/11/81: El Salvador's Atlacatl Battalion begins a 6-day offensive sweep against guerrilla strongholds in Morazán."

—*From the U.S. Embassy "Chronology of Events."*

"The department of Morazán, one of the country's most embattled areas, was the scene of another armed forces operation in December, the fourth in Morazán during 1981. . . . The hamlet of Mozote was completely wiped out. For this reason, the several massacres which occurred in the same area at the same time are collectively known as the 'Mozote massacre.' The apparent sole survivor from Mozote, Rufina Amaya, thirty-eight years old, escaped by hiding behind trees near the house where she and the other women had been imprisoned. She has testified that on Friday, December 11, troops arrived and began taking people from their homes at about 5 in the morning. . . . At noon, the men were blindfolded and killed in the town's center. Among them was Amaya's husband, who was nearly blind. In the early afternoon the young women were taken to the hills nearby, where they were raped, then killed and burned. The old women were taken next and shot. . . . From her hiding place, Amaya heard soldiers discuss choking the children to death; subsequently she heard the children calling for help, but no shots. Among the children murdered were three of Amaya's, all under ten years of age. . . . It should be stressed that the villagers in the area had been warned of the impending military operation by the FMLN and some did leave. Those who chose to stay, such as the evangelical Protestants and others, considered themselves neutral in the conflict and friendly with the army. According to Rufina Amaya, 'Because we knew the Army people, we felt safe.' Her husband, she said, had been on good terms with the local military and even had what she called 'a military safe-conduct.' Amaya and other survivors [of the nine hamlets in which the killing took place] accused the Atlacatl Battalion of a major role in the killing of civilians in the Mozote area."

—From the July 20 1982 Supplement to the "Report on Human Rights in El Salvador" prepared by Americas Watch Committee and the American Civil Liberties Union.

At the time I was in El Salvador, six months after the events referred to as the Mozote massacre and a month or so before President Reagan's July 1982 certification that sufficient progress was being made in specified areas ("human rights," and "land reform," and "the initiation of a democratic political process," phrases so remote *in situ* as to render them hallucinatory) to qualify El Salvador for continuing aid, a major offensive was taking place in Morazán, up in the mean hill country between the garrison town of San Francisco Gotera and the Honduran border. This June 1982 fighting was referred to by both sides as the heaviest of the war to date, but actual information, on this as on all subjects in San Salvador, was hard to come by.

Reports drifted back. The Atlacatl, which was trained by American advisers in 1981, was definitely up there again, as were two other battalions, the Atonal, trained, like the Atlacatl, by Americans in El Salvador, and the Ramón Belloso, just back from training at Fort Bragg. Every morning COPREFA, the press office at the Ministry of Defense, reported many FMLN casualties but few government. Every afternoon Radio Venceremos, the clandestine guerrilla radio station, reported many government casualties but few FMLN. The only way to get any sense of what was happening was to go up there, but Morazán was hard to reach: a key bridge between San Salvador and the eastern half of the country, the Puente de Oro on the Río Lempa, had been dynamited by the FMLN in October 1981, and to reach San Francisco Gotera it was now necessary either to cross the Lempa on a railroad bridge or to fly, which meant going out to the military airport, Ilopango, and trying to get one of the seven-passenger prop planes that the Gutierrez Flying Service operated between Ilopango and a grassy field outside San Miguel. At San Miguel one could sometimes get a taxi willing to go on up to San Francisco Gotera, or a bus, the problem with a bus being that even a roadblock that ended well (no one killed or detained) could take hours, while every passenger was questioned. Between San Miguel and Gotera, moreover, there was a further problem, another blown bridge, this one on the Río Seco, which was *seco* enough in the dry months but often impassable in the wet.

June was wet. The Río Seco seemed doubtful. Everything about the day ahead, on the morning I started for Gotera, seemed doubtful, and that I set out on such a venture with a real lightening of the spirit suggests to me now how powerfully I wanted to get out of San Salvador, to spend a day free of its ambiguous tension, its overcast, its mood of wary somnambulism. It was only a trip of perhaps eighty miles, but getting there took most of the morning. There was, first of all, the wait on the runway at Ilopango while the pilot tried to get the engines to catch. "*Cinco minutos*," he kept saying, and, as a wrench was produced, "*Momentito*." Thunderclouds were massing on the mountains to the east. Rain spattered the fuselage. The plane was full, seven paying passengers at ninety-five *colones* the round trip, and we watched the tinkering without comment until one and finally both of the engines turned over.

Once in the air I was struck, as always in Salvador, by the miniature aspect of the country, an entire republic smaller than some California counties (smaller than San Diego County, smaller than Kern or Inyo, smaller by two-and-a-half times than San Bernardino), the very circumstance that has encouraged the illusion that the place can be managed, salvaged, a kind of pilot project, like TVA. There below us in a twenty-five-minute flight lay half the country, a landscape already densely green from the rains that had begun in May, intensely cultivated, deceptively rich, the coffee spreading down every ravine, the volcanic ranges looming abruptly and then receding. I watched the slopes of the mountains for signs of fighting but saw none. I watched for the hydroelectric works on the Lempa but saw only the blown bridge.

There were four of us on the flight that morning who wanted to go on to Gotera, my husband and I and Christopher Dickey from *The Washington Post* and Joseph Harmes from *Newsweek*, and when the plane set down on the grass strip outside San Miguel a deal was struck with a taxi driver willing to take us at least to the Río Seco. We shared the taxi as far as San Miguel with a local woman who, although she and I sat on a single bucket seat, did not speak, only stared straight ahead, clutching her bag with one hand and trying with the other to keep her skirt pulled down over her black lace slip. When she got out at San Miguel there remained in the taxi a trace of her perfume, Arpège.

In San Miguel the streets showed the marks of January's fighting, and many structures were boarded up, abandoned. There had been a passable motel in San Miguel, but the owners had managed to leave the country. There had been a passable place to eat in San Miguel, but no more. Occasional troop trucks hurtled past, presumably returning empty from the front, and we all made note of them, dutifully. The heat rose.

Sweat from my hand kept blurring my tally of empty troop trucks, and I copied it on a clean page, painstakingly, as if it mattered.

The heat up here was drier than that in the capital, harsher, dustier, and by now we were resigned to it, resigned to the jolting of the taxi, resigned to the frequent occasions on which we were required to stop, get out, present our identification (carefully, reaching slowly into an outer pocket, every move calculated not to startle the soldiers, many of whom seemed barely pubescent, with the M-16s), and wait while the taxi was searched. Some of the younger soldiers wore crucifixes wrapped with bright yarn, the pink and green of the yarn stained now with dust and sweat. The taxi driver was perhaps twenty years older than most of these soldiers, a stocky, well-settled citizen wearing expensive sunglasses, but at each roadblock, in a motion so abbreviated as to be almost imperceptible, he would touch each of the two rosaries that hung from the rearview mirror and cross himself.

By the time we reached the Río Seco the question of whether or not we could cross it seemed insignificant, another minor distraction in a day that had begun at six and was now, before nine, already less a day than a way of being alive. We would try, the driver announced, to ford the river, which appeared that day to be running shallow and relatively fast over an unpredictable bed of sand and mud. We stood for a while on the bank and watched a man with an earthmover and winch try again and again to hook up his equipment to a truck that had foundered midstream. Small boys dove repeatedly with hooks, and repeatedly surfaced, unsuccessful. It did not seem entirely promising, but there it was, and there, in due time, we were: in the river, first following the sandbar in a wide crescent, then off the bar, stuck, the engine dead. The taxi rocked gently in the current. The water bubbled inch by inch through the floorboards. There were women bathing naked in the shallows, and they paid no attention to the earthmover, the small boys, the half-submerged taxi, the *gringos* inside it. As we waited for our turn with the earthmover it occurred to me that fording the river in the morning meant only that we were going to have to ford it again in the afternoon, when the earthmover might or might not be around, but this was thinking ahead, and out of synch with the day at hand.

When I think now of that day in Gotera I think mainly of waiting, hanging around, waiting outside the *cuartel* ("COMANDO," the signs read on the gates, and "BOINAS VERDES," with a green beret) and waiting outside the church and waiting outside the Cine Morazán, where the posters promised *Fright* and *The Abominable Snowman* and the open lobby was lined with .50-caliber machine guns and 120-mm. mobile mortars. There were soldiers billeted in the Cine Morazán, and a few of them kicked a soccer ball, idly, among the mortars. Others joked among themselves at the corner, outside the saloon, and flirted with the women selling Coca-Cola in the stalls between the Cine Morazán and the parish house. The parish house and the church and the stalls and the saloon and the Cine Morazán and the *cuartel* all faced one another, across what was less a square than a dusty widening in the road, an arrangement that lent Gotera a certain proscenium aspect. Any event at all—the arrival of an armored personnel carrier, say, or a funeral procession outside the church—tended to metamorphose instantly into an opera, with all players onstage: the Soldiers of the Garrison, the Young Ladies of the Town, the Vendors, the Priests, the Mourners, and, since we were onstage as well, a dissonant and provocative element, the *norteamericanos*, in *norteamericano* costume, old Abercrombie khakis here, Adidas sneakers there, a Lone Star Beer cap.

We stood in the sun and tried to avoid adverse attention. We drank Coca-Cola and made surreptitious notes. We looked for the priests in the parish office but found only the receptionist, a dwarf. We presented our credentials again and again at the *cuartel*, trying to see the colonel who could give us permission to go up the few kilometers to where the fighting was, but the colonel was out, the colonel would be back, the colonel was delayed. The young officer in charge during the colonel's absence could not give us permission, but he had graduated from the Escuela Militar in one of the classes trained in the spring of 1982 at Fort Benning ("Mar-vel-*ous!*" was his impression of Fort Benning) and seemed at least amenable to us as Americans. Possibly there would be a patrol going up. Possibly we could join it.

In the end no patrol went up and the colonel never

came back (the reason the colonel never came back is that he was killed that afternoon, in a helicopter crash near the Honduran border, but we did not learn this in Gotera) and nothing came of the day but overheard rumors, indefinite observations, fragments of information that might or might not fit into a pattern we did not perceive. One of the six A-37B Dragonfly attack jets that the United States had delivered just that week to Ilopango screamed low overhead, then disappeared. A company of soldiers burst through the *cuartel* gates and double-timed to the river, but when we caught up they were only bathing, shedding their uniforms and splashing in the shallow water. On the bluff above the river work was being completed on a helipad that was said to cover two mass graves of dead soldiers, but the graves were no longer apparent. The taxi driver heard, from the soldiers with whom he talked while he waited (talked and played cards and ate tortillas and sardines and listened to rock-and-roll on the taxi radio), that two whole companies were missing in action, lost or dead somewhere in the hills, but this was received information, and equivocal.

In some ways the least equivocal fact of the day was the single body we had seen that morning on the road between the Río Seco and Gotera, near San Carlos, the naked corpse of a man about thirty with a clean bullet-hole drilled neatly between his eyes. He could have been stripped by whoever killed him or, since this was a country in which clothes were too valuable to leave on the dead, by someone who happened past: there was no way of telling. In any case his genitals had been covered with a leafy branch, presumably by the *campesinos* who were even then digging a grave. A *subversivo*, the driver thought, because there was no family in evidence (to be related to someone killed in El Salvador is a prima facie death warrant, and families tend to vanish), but all anyone in Gotera seemed to know was that there had been another body at precisely that place the morning before, and five others before that. One of the priests in Gotera had happened to see the body the morning before, but when he drove past San Carlos later in the day the body had been buried. It was agreed that someone was trying to make a point. The point was unclear.

We spent an hour or so that day with the priests, or with two of them, both Irish, and two of the nuns, one Irish and one American, all of whom lived together in the parish house facing the *cuartel* in a situation that remains in my mind as the one actual instance I have witnessed of grace not simply under pressure but under siege. Except for the American, Sister Phyllis, who had arrived only a few months before, they had all been in Gotera a long time, twelve years, nine years, long enough to have established among themselves a grave companionableness, a courtesy and good humor that made the courtyard porch where we sat with them seem civilization's last stand in Morazán, which in certain ways it was.

The light on the porch was cool and aqueous, filtered through ferns and hibiscus, and there were old wicker rockers and a map of PARROQUIA SAN FRANCISCO GOTERA and a wooden table with a typewriter, a can of Planter's Mixed Nuts, copies of *Lives of the Saints: Illustrated* and *The Rules of the Secular Franciscan Order*. In the shadows beyond the table was a battered refrigerator from which, after a while, one of the priests got bottles of Pilsener beer, and we sat in the sedative half-light and drank the cold beer and talked in a desultory way about nothing in particular, about the situation, but no solutions.

These were not people much given to solutions, to abstracts: their lives were grounded in the specific. There had been the funeral that morning of a parishioner who had died in the night of cerebral hemorrhage. There had been the two children who died that week, of diarrhea, dehydration, in the squatter camps outside town where some 12,000 refugees were then gathered, many of them ill. There was no medicine in the camps. There was no water anywhere, and had been none since around the time of the election, when the tank that supplied Gotera with water had been dynamited. Five or six weeks after the tank was blown the rains had begun, which was bad in one way, because the rain washed out the latrines at the camps, but good in another, because at the parish house they were no longer dependent entirely on water from the river, soupy with bacteria and amoebae and worms. "We have the roof water now," Sister Jean, the Irish nun, said. "Much cleaner. It's greenish yellow, the river water, we only use it for the toilets."

There had been, they agreed, fewer dead around

since the election, fewer bodies, they thought, than in the capital, but as they began reminding one another of this body or that there still seemed to have been quite a few. They spoke of these bodies in the matter-of-fact way that they might have spoken, in another kind of parish, of confirmation candidates, or cases of croup. There had been the few up the road, the two at Yoloaiquin. Of course there had been the forty-eight near Barrios, but Barrios was in April. "A *guardia* was killed last Wednesday," one of them recalled.

"Thursday."

"Was it Thursday then, Jerry?"

"A sniper."

"That's what I thought. A sniper."

We left the parish house that day only because rain seemed about to fall, and it was clear that the Río Seco had to be crossed now or perhaps not for days. The priests kept a guest book, and I thought as I signed it that I would definitely come back to this porch, come back with antibiotics and Scotch and time to spend, but I did not get back, and some weeks after I left El Salvador I heard in a third-hand way that the parish house had been at least temporarily abandoned, that the priests, who had been under threats and pressure from the garrison, had somehow been forced to leave Gotera. I recalled that on the day before I left El Salvador Deane Hinton had asked me, when I mentioned Gotera, if I had seen the priests, and had expressed concern for their situation. He was particularly concerned about the American, Sister Phyllis (an American nun in a parish under siege in a part of the country even then under attack from American A-37Bs was nothing the

American embassy needed in those last delicate weeks before certification), and had at some point expressed this concern to the *comandante* at the garrison. The *comandante*, he said, had been surprised to learn the nationalities of the nuns and priests; he had thought them French, because the word used to describe them was always "Franciscan." This was one of those occasional windows that open onto the heart of El Salvador and then close, a glimpse of the impenetrable interior.

At the time I was in El Salvador the hostilities at hand were referred to by those reporters still in the country as "the number-four war," after Beirut, Iran-Iraq, and the aftermath of the Falklands. So many reporters had in fact abandoned the Hotel Camino Real in San Salvador (gone home for a while, or gone to the Intercontinental in Managua, or gone to whatever hotels they frequented in Guatemala and Panama and Tegucigalpa) that the dining room had discontinued its breakfast buffet, a fact often remarked upon: no breakfast buffet meant no action, little bang-bang, a period of editorial indifference in which stories were filed and held, and film rarely made the network news. "Get an NBC crew up from the Falklands, we might get the buffet back," they would say, and, "It hots up a little, we could have the midnight movies." It seemed that when the networks arrived in force they brought movies down, and showed them at midnight on their video recorders, *Apocalypse Now*, and Woody Allen's *Bananas*.

Meanwhile only the regulars were there. "Are you going out today?" they would say to one another at breakfast, and, "This might not be a bad day to look around." The Avis counter in the bar supplied signs reading "PRENSA INTERNACIONAL" with every car and van, and modified its insurance agreements with a typed clause excluding damage incurred by terrorists. The American embassy delivered translated transcripts of Radio Venceremos, prepared by the CIA in Panama. The COPREFA office at the Ministry of Defense sent over "urgent" notices, taped to the front desk, announcing events specifically devised, in those weeks before certification, for the American press: the ceremonial transfer of land titles, and the ritual display of "defectors," terrified-looking men who were reported in *La Prensa Gráfica* to have "abandoned the ranks of subversion, weary of so many lies and false promises."

A handful of reporters continued to cover these events, particularly if they were staged in provincial garrisons and offered the possibility of action en route, but action was less than certain, and the situation less accessible than it had seemed in the days of the breakfast buffet. The American advisers would talk to no one, although occasionally a reporter could find a few drinking at the Sheraton on Saturday night and initiate a little general conversation. (That the American advisers were still billeted at the Sheraton struck me as somewhat perverse, particularly because I knew that the embassy had moved its visiting AID people to a guarded house in San Benito. "Frankly, I'd rather stay at the Sheraton," an AID man had told me. "But since the two union guys got killed at the Sheraton, they want us here.") The era in which the guerrillas could be found just by going out on the highway had largely ended; the only certain way to spend time with them now was to cross into their territory from Honduras, through contact with the leadership in Mexico. This was a process that tended to discourage day-tripping, and in any case it was no longer a war in which the dateline "SOMEWHERE BEHIND GUERRILLA LINES, EL SALVADOR" was presumed automatically to illuminate much at all.

Everyone had already spent time, too, with the available government players, most of whom had grown so practiced in the process that their interviews were now performances, less apt to be reported than reviewed, and analyzed for subtle changes in delivery. Roberto D'Aubuisson had even taken part, wittingly or unwittingly, in an actual performance: a scene shot by a Danish film crew on location in Haiti and El Salvador for a movie about a foreign correspondent, in which the actor playing the correspondent "interviewed" D'Aubuisson, on camera, in his office. This Danish crew treated the Camino Real not only as a normal location hotel (the star, for example, was the only person I ever saw swim in the Camino Real pool) but also as a story element, on one occasion shooting a scene in the bar, which lent daily life during their stay a peculiar extra color. They left San Salvador without making it entirely clear whether or not they had ever told D'Aubuisson it was just a movie.

Aт twenty-two minutes past midnight on Saturday June 19, 1982, there was a major earthquake in El Salvador, one that collapsed shacks and set off landslides and injured several hundred people but killed only about a dozen (I say "about" a dozen because figures on this, as on everything else in Salvador, varied), surprisingly few for an earthquake of this one's apparent intensity (Cal Tech registered it at 7.0 on the Richter scale, Berkeley at 7.4) and length, thirty-seven seconds. For the several hours that preceded the earthquake I had been seized by the kind of amorphous bad mood that my grandmother believed an adjunct of what is called in California "earthquake weather," a sultriness, a stillness, an unnatural light; the jitters. In fact there was no particular prescience about my bad mood, since it is always earthquake weather in San Salvador, and the jitters are endemic.

I recall having come back to the Camino Real about ten-thirty that Friday night, after dinner in a Mexican restaurant on the Paseo Escalón with a Salvadoran painter named Victor Barriere, who had said, when we met at a party a few days before, that he was interested in talking to Americans because they so often came and went with no understanding of the country and its history. Victor Barriere could offer, he explained, a special perspective on the country and its history, because he was a grandson of the late General Maximiliano Hernández Martínez, the dictator of El Salvador between 1931 and 1944 and the author of what Salvadorans still call *la matanza*, the massacre, or "killing," those weeks in 1932 when the government killed uncountable thousands of citizens, a lesson. ("Uncountable" because estimates of those killed vary from six or seven thousand to thirty thousand. Even higher figures are heard in Salvador, but, as Thomas P. Anderson pointed out in *Matanza: El Salvador's Communist Revolt of 1932*, "Salvadorans, like medieval people, tend to use numbers like fifty thousand simply to indicate a great number—statistics are not their strong point.")

As it happened I had been interested for some years in General Martínez, the spirit of whose regime would seem to have informed Gabriel García Márquez's *The Autumn of the Patriarch*. This original patriarch, who was murdered in exile in Honduras in 1966, was a rather sinister visionary who entrenched the military in Salvadoran life, was said to have held séances in the Casa Presidencial, and conducted both the country's and his own affairs along lines dictated by eccentric insights, which he sometimes shared by radio with the remaining citizens:

> "It is good that children go barefoot. That way they can better receive the beneficial effluvia of the planet, the vibrations of the earth. Plants and animals don't use shoes."

"Biologists have discovered only five senses. But in reality there are ten. Hunger, thirst, procreation, urination, and bowel movements are the senses not included in the lists of biologists."

I had first come across this side of General Martínez in the United States Government Printing Office's *Area Handbook for El Salvador*, a generally straightforward volume ("designed to be useful to military and other personnel who need a convenient compilation of basic facts") in which, somewhere between the basic facts about General Martínez's program for building schools and the basic facts about General Martínez's program for increasing exports, there appears this sentence: "He kept bottles of colored water that he dispensed as cures for almost any disease, including cancer and heart trouble, and relied on complex magical formulas for the solution of national problems." This sentence springs from the *Area Handbook for El Salvador* as if printed in neon, and is followed by one even more arresting: "During an epidemic of smallpox in the capital, he attempted to halt its spread by stringing the city with a web of colored lights."

Not a night passed in San Salvador when I did not imagine it strung with those colored lights, and I asked Victor Barriere what it had been like to grow up as the grandson of General Martínez. Victor Barriere had studied for a while in the United States, at the San Diego campus of the University of California, and he spoke perfect unaccented English, with the slightly formal constructions of the foreign speaker, in a fluted, melodic voice that seemed always to suggest a higher reasonableness. The general had been, he said, sometimes misunderstood. Very strong men often were. Certain excesses had been inevitable. Someone had to take charge. "It was sometimes strange going to school with boys whose fathers my grandfather had ordered shot," he allowed, but he remembered his grandfather mainly as a "forceful" man, a man "capable of inspiring great loyalty," a theosophist from whom it had been possible to learn an appreciation of "the classics," "a sense of history," "the Germans." The Germans especially had influenced Victor Barriere's sense of history. "When you've read Schopenhauer, Nietzsche, what's happened here, what's happening here, well . . ."

Victor Barriere had shrugged, and the subject changed, although only fractionally, since El Salvador is one of those places in the world where there is just one subject, the situation, the *problema*, its various facets presented over and over again, as on a stereopticon. One turn, and the facet was former ambassador Robert White: "A real jerk." Another, the murder in March of 1980 of Archbishop Oscar Arnulfo Romero: "A real bigot." At first I thought he meant whoever stood outside an open door of the chapel in which the Archbishop was saying mass and drilled him through the heart with a .22-caliber dumdum bullet, but he did not: "Listening to that man on the radio every Sunday," he said, "was like listening to Adolf Hitler or Benito Mussolini." In any case: "We don't really know who killed him, do we? It could have been the right . . ." He drew the words out, *cantabile*. "Or . . .

it could have been the left. We have to ask ourselves, who gained? Think about it, Joan."

I said nothing. I wanted only for dinner to end. Victor Barriere had brought a friend along, a young man from Chalatenango whom he was teaching to paint, and the friend brightened visibly when we stood up. He was eighteen years old and spoke no English and had sat through the dinner in polite misery. "He can't even speak Spanish properly," Victor Barriere said, in front of him. "However. If he were cutting cane in Chalatenango, he'd be taken by the Army and killed. If he were out on the street here he'd be killed. So. He comes every day to my studio, he learns to be a primitive painter, and I keep him from getting killed. It's better for him, don't you agree?"

I said that I agreed. The two of them were going back to the house Victor Barriere shared with his mother, a diminutive woman he addressed as "Mommy," the daughter of General Martínez, and after I dropped them there it occurred to me that this was the first time in my life that I had been in the presence of obvious "material" and felt no professional exhilaration at all, only personal dread. One of the most active death squads now operating in El Salvador calls itself the Maximiliano Hernández Martínez Brigade, but I had not asked the grandson about that.

In spite of or perhaps because of the fact that San Salvador had been for more than two years under an almost constant state of siege, a city in which arbitrary

detention had been legalized (Revolutionary Govern-
ing Junta Decree 507), curfew violations had been
known to end in death, and many people did not leave
their houses after dark, a certain limited frivolity still
obtained. When I got back to the Camino Real after
dinner with Victor Barriere that Friday night there
was for example a private party at the pool, with live
music, dancing, an actual conga line.

There were also a number of people in the bar, many
of them watching, on television monitors, "Señorita El
Salvador 1982," the selection of El Salvador's entry in
"Señorita Universo 1982," scheduled for July 1982 in
Lima. Something about "Señorita Universo" struck a
familiar note, and then I recalled that the Miss Universe
contest itself had been held in San Salvador in 1975, and
had ended in what might have been considered a predictable way, with student protests about the money
the government was spending on the contest, and the
government's predictable response, which was to shoot
some of the students on the street and disappear others.
(*Desaparecer*, or "disappear," is in Spanish both an
intransitive and a transitive verb, and this flexibility has
been adopted by those speaking English in El Salvador,
as in *John Sullivan was disappeared from the Sheraton;
the government disappeared the students*, there being
no equivalent situation, and so no equivalent word, in
English-speaking cultures.)

No mention of "Señorita Universo 1975" dampened
"Señorita El Salvador 1982," which, by the time I got
upstairs, had reached the point when each of the finalists was asked to pick a question from a basket and

answer it. The questions had to do with the hopes and dreams of the contestants, and the answers ran to "*Dios,*" "*Paz,*" "El Salvador." A local entertainer wearing a white dinner jacket and a claret-colored bow tie sang "The Impossible Dream," in Spanish. The judges began their deliberations, and the moment of decision arrived: Señorita El Salvador 1982 would be Señorita San Vicente, Miss Jeannette Marroquín, who was several inches taller than the other finalists, and more *gringa*-looking. The four runners-up reacted, on the whole, with rather less grace than is the custom on these occasions, and it occurred to me that this was a contest in which winning meant more than a scholarship or a screen test or a new wardrobe; winning here could mean the difference between life and casual death, a provisional safe-conduct not only for the winner but for her entire family.

"God damn it, he cut inaugural ribbons, he showed himself large as life in public taking on the risks of power as he had never done in more peaceful times, what the hell, he played endless games of dominoes with my lifetime friend General Rodrigo de Aguilar and my old friend the minister of health who were the only ones who . . . dared ask him to receive in a special audience the beauty queen of the poor, an incredible creature from that miserable wallow we call the dogfight district. . . . I'll not only receive her in a special audience but I'll dance the first waltz with her, by God, have them write it up in the newspapers, he ordered, this kind of crap makes a big hit with the poor. Yet, the night after the audience, he commented with a certain bitterness to General Rodrigo de Aguilar that the queen of the poor wasn't even worth dancing with, that she was as common as so many other slum Manuela Sánchezes with her nymph's dress of muslin petticoats and the gilt crown with artificial jewels and a rose in her hand under the watchful eye of a mother who looked after her as if she were made of gold, so he gave her everything she wanted which was only electricity and running water for the dogfight district. . . ."

That is Gabriel García Márquez, *The Autumn of the Patriarch*. On this evening that began with the grandson of General Maximiliano Hernández Martínez and progressed to "Señorita El Salvador 1982" and ended, at 12:22 A.M., with the earthquake, I began to see Gabriel García Márquez in a new light, as a social realist.

There were a number of metaphors to be found in this earthquake, not the least of them being that the one major building to suffer extensive damage happened also to be the major building most specifically and elaborately designed to withstand earthquakes, the American embassy. When this embassy was built, in 1965, the idea was that it would remain fluid under stress, its deep pilings shifting and sliding on Teflon pads, but over the past few years, as shelling the embassy came to be a favorite way of expressing dissatisfaction on all sides, the structure became so fortified—the steel exterior walls, the wet sandbags around the gun emplacements on the roof, the bomb shelter dug out underneath—as to render it rigid. The ceiling fell in Deane Hinton's office that night. Pipes burst on the third floor, flooding everything below. The elevator was disabled, the commissary a sea of shattered glass.

The Hotel Camino Real, on the other hand, which would appear to have been thrown together in the insouciant tradition of most tropical construction, did a considerable amount of rolling (I recall crouching under a door frame in my room on the seventh floor and watching, through the window, the San Salvador volcano appear to rock from left to right), but when the wrenching stopped and candles were found and everyone got downstairs nothing was broken, not even the glasses behind the bar. There was no electricity, but there was often no electricity. There were sporadic bursts of machine-gun fire on the street (this had made getting downstairs more problematic than it might have been, since the emergency stairway was exposed to the street), but sporadic bursts of machine-gun fire on the street were not entirely unusual in San Salvador. ("Sometimes it happens when it rains," someone from the embassy had told me about this phenomenon. "They get excited.") On the whole it was business as usual at the Camino Real, particularly in the discothèque off the lobby, where, by the time I got downstairs, an emergency generator seemed already to have been activated, waiters in black cowboy hats darted about the dance floor carrying drinks, and dancing continued, to Jerry Lee Lewis's "Great Balls of Fire."

Actual information was hard to come by in El Salvador, perhaps because this is not a culture in which a high value is placed on the definite. The only hard facts on the earthquake, for example, arrived at the Camino Real that night from New York, on the AP wire, which reported the Cal Tech reading of 7.0 Richter on an earthquake centered in the Pacific some sixty miles south of San Salvador. Over the next few days, as damage reports appeared in the local papers, the figure varied. One day the earthquake had been a 7.0 Richter, another day a 6.8. By Tuesday it was again a 7 in *La Prensa Gráfica*, but on a different scale altogether, not the Richter but the Modified Mercalli.

All numbers in El Salvador tended to materialize and vanish and rematerialize in a different form, as if numbers denoted only the "use" of numbers, an intention, a wish, a recognition that someone, somewhere, for whatever reason, needed to hear the ineffable expressed as a number. At any given time in El Salvador a great deal of what goes on is considered ineffable, and the use of numbers in this context tends to frustrate people who try to understand them literally, rather than as propositions to be floated, "heard," "mentioned." There was the case of the March 28 1982 election, about which there continued into that summer the rather scholastic argument first posed by *Central American Studies*, the publication of the Jesuit university in San Salvador: Had it taken an average of 2.5 minutes to cast a vote, or less? Could each ballot box hold 500 ballots, or more? The numbers were eerily Salvadoran. There were said to be 1.3 million people eligible to vote on March 28, but 1.5 million people were said to have voted. These 1.5 million people were said, in turn, to represent not 115 percent of the 1.3 million eligible voters but 80 percent (or, on another float, "62–68 percent") of the eligible voters, who accordingly no longer numbered 1.3 million, but a larger number. In any case no one really knew how many eligible voters there were in El Salvador, or even how many people. In any case it had seemed necessary to provide a number. In any case the election was over, a success, *la solución pacífica*.

Similarly, there was the question of how much money had left the country for Miami since 1979: Deane Hinton, in March of 1982, estimated $740 million. The Salvadoran minister of planning estimated, the same month, twice that. I recall asking President Magaña, when he happened to say that he had gone to lunch every Tuesday for the past ten years with the officers of the Central Reserve Bank of El Salvador, which reviews the very export and import transactions through which money traditionally leaves troubled countries, how much he thought was gone. "You hear figures mentioned," he said. I asked what figures he heard mentioned at these Tuesday lunches. "The figure they mentioned is six hundred million," he said. He watched as I wrote that down, *600,000,000, central bank El Salvador*. "The figure the Federal Reserve in New York mentioned," he added, "is one thousand million." He watched as I wrote that down too, *1,000,000,000, Fed NY*. "Those people don't want to stay for life in Miami," he said then, but this did not entirely address the question, nor was it meant to.

Not only numbers but names are understood locally to have only a situational meaning, and the change of a name is meant to be accepted as a change in the nature of the thing named. ORDEN, for example, the paramilitary organization formally founded in 1968 to function, along classic patronage lines, as the government's eyes and ears in the countryside, no longer exists as ORDEN, or the Organización Democrática Nacionalista, but as the Frente Democrática Nacionalista, a transubstantiation noted only cryptically in the State Department's official "justification" for the January 28 1982 certification: "The Salvadoran government, since the overthrow of General Romero, has taken explicit actions to end human rights abuses. The paramilitary organization 'ORDEN' has been outlawed, *although some of its former members may still be active*." (Italics added.)

This tactic of solving a problem by changing its name is by no means limited to the government. The small office on the archdiocese grounds where the scrapbooks of the dead are kept is still called, by virtually everyone in San Salvador, "the Human Rights Commission" (Comisión de los Derechos Humanos), but in fact both the Human Rights Commission and

Socorro Jurídico, the archdiocesan legal aid office, were ordered in the spring of 1982 to vacate the church property, and, in the local way, did so: everything pretty much stayed in place, but the scrapbooks of the dead were thereafter kept, officially, in the "Oficina de Tutela Legal" of the "Comisión Arquidiocesana de Justicia y Paz." (This "Human Rights Commission," in any case, is not to be confused with the Salvadoran government's "Commission on Human Rights," the formation of which was announced the day before a scheduled meeting between President Magaña and Ronald Reagan. This official *comisión* is a seven-member panel notable for its inclusion of Colonel Carlos Reynaldo López Nuila, the director of the National Police.) This renaming was referred to as a "reorganization," which is one of many words in El Salvador that tend to signal the presence of the ineffable.

Other such words are "improvement," "perfection" (reforms are never abandoned or ignored, only "perfected" or "improved"), and that favorite from other fronts, "pacification." Language has always been used a little differently in this part of the world (an apparent statement of fact often expresses something only wished for, or something that might be true, a story, as in García Márquez's *many years later, as he faced the firing squad, Colonel Aureliano Buendía was to remember that distant afternoon when his father took him to discover ice*), but "improvement" and "perfection" and "pacification" derive from another tradition. Language as it is now used in El Salvador is the language of advertising, of persuasion, the product being one or another of the *soluciones* crafted in Washington or Panama or Mexico, which is part of the place's pervasive obscenity.

This language is shared by Salvadorans and Americans, as if a linguistic deal had been cut. "Perhaps the most striking measure of progress [in El Salvador]," Assistant Secretary of State Thomas Enders was able to say in August of 1982 in a speech at the Commonwealth Club in San Francisco, "is the transformation of the military from an institution dedicated to the status quo to one that spearheads land reform and supports constitutional democracy." Thomas Enders was able to say this precisely because the Salvadoran minister of defense, General José Guillermo García, had so superior a dedication to his own status quo that he played the American card as Roberto D'Aubuisson did not, played the game, played ball, understood the importance to Americans of symbolic action: the importance of letting the Americans have their land reform program, the importance of letting the Americans pretend that while "democracy in El Salvador" may remain "a slender reed" (that was Elliott Abrams in *The New York Times*), the situation is one in which "progress" is measurable ("the minister of defense has ordered that all violations of citizens' rights be stopped immediately," the State Department noted on the occasion of the July 1982 certification, a happy ending); the importance of giving the Americans an acceptable president, Alvaro Magaña, and of pretending that this acceptable president was in fact commander-in-chief of the armed forces, *el generalísimo* as *la solución*.

La solución changed with the market. Pacification, although those places pacified turned out to be in need of repeated pacification, was *la solución*. The use of the word "negotiations," however abstract that use may have been, was *la solución*. The election, although it ended with the ascension of a man, Roberto D'Aubuisson, essentially hostile to American policy, was *la solución* for Americans. The land reform program, grounded as it was in political rather than economic reality, was *la solución* as symbol. "It has not been a total economic success," Peter Askin, the AID director working with the government on the program, told *The New York Times* in August 1981, "but up to this point it has been a political success. I'm firm on that. There does seem to be a direct correlation between the agrarian reforms and the peasants not having become more radicalized." The land reform program, in other words, was based on the principle of buying off, buying time, giving a little to gain a lot, *minifundismo* in support of *latifundismo*, which, in a country where the left had no interest in keeping the peasants less "radicalized" and the right remained unconvinced that these peasants could not simply be eliminated, rendered it a program about which only Americans could be truly enthusiastic, less a "reform" than an exercise in public relations.

Even *la verdad*, the truth, was a degenerated phrase

in El Salvador: on my first evening in the country I was asked by a Salvadoran woman at an embassy party what I hoped to find out in El Salvador. I said that ideally I hoped to find out *la verdad*, and she beamed approvingly. Other journalists, she said, did not want *la verdad*. She called over two friends, who also approved: no one told *la verdad*. If I wrote *la verdad* it would be good for El Salvador. I realized that I had stumbled into a code, that these women used *la verdad* as it was used on the bumper stickers favored that spring and summer by ARENA people. "JOURNALISTS, TELL THE TRUTH!" the bumper stickers warned in Spanish, and they meant the truth according to Roberto D'Aubuisson.

In the absence of information (and the presence, often, of disinformation) even the most apparently straightforward event takes on, in El Salvador, elusive shadows, like a fragment of retrieved legend. On the afternoon that I was in San Francisco Gotera trying to see the commander of the garrison there, this *comandante*, Colonel Salvador Beltrán Luna, was killed, or was generally believed to have been killed, in the crash of a Hughes 500-D helicopter. The crash of a helicopter in a war zone would seem to lend itself to only a limited number of interpretations (the helicopter was shot down, or the helicopter suffered mechanical failure, are the two that come to mind), but the crash of this particular helicopter became, like everything else in Salvador, an occasion of rumor, doubt, suspicion, conflicting reports, and finally a kind of listless uneasiness.

The crash occurred either near the Honduran border in Morazán or, the speculation went, actually in Honduras. There were or were not four people aboard the helicopter: the pilot, a bodyguard, Colonel Beltrán Luna, and the assistant secretary of defense, Colonel Francisco Adolfo Castillo. At first all four were dead. A day later only three were dead: Radio Venceremos broadcast news of Colonel Castillo (followed a few days later by a voice resembling that of Colonel Castillo), not dead but a prisoner, or said to be a prisoner, or perhaps only claiming to be a prisoner. A day or so later another of the dead materialized, or appeared to: the pilot was, it seemed, neither dead nor a prisoner but hospitalized, incommunicado.

Questions about what actually happened to (or on, or after the crash of, or after the clandestine landing of) this helicopter provided table talk for days (one morning the newspapers emphasized that the Hughes 500-D had been *comprado en Guatemala*, bought in Guatemala, a detail so solid in this otherwise vaporous story that it suggested rumors yet unheard, intrigues yet unimagined), and remained unresolved at the time I left. At one point I asked President Magaña, who had talked to the pilot, what had happened. "They don't say," he said. Was Colonel Castillo a prisoner? "I read that in the paper, yes." Was Colonel Beltrán Luna dead? "I have that impression." Was the bodyguard dead? "Well, the pilot said he saw someone lying on the ground, either dead or unconscious, he doesn't know, but he believes it may have been Castillo's security man, yes." Where exactly had the helicopter crashed? "I didn't ask him." I looked at President Magaña, and he shrugged. "This is very delicate," he said. "I have a problem there. I'm supposed to be the commander-in-chief, so if I ask him, he should tell me. But he might say he's not going to tell me, then I would have to arrest him. So I don't ask." This is in many ways the standard development of a story in El Salvador, and is also illustrative of the position of the provisional president of El Salvador.

News of the outside world drifted in only fitfully, and in peculiar details. *La Prensa Gráfica* carried a regular column of news from San Francisco, California, and I recall reading in this column one morning that a man identified as a former president of the Bohemian Club had died, at age seventy-two, at his home in Tiburon. Most days *The Miami Herald* came in at some point, and sporadically *The New York Times* or *The Washington Post*, but there would be days when nothing came in at all, and I would find myself rifling back sports sections of *The Miami Herald* for installments of *Chrissie: My Own Story*, by Chris Evert Lloyd with Neil Amdur, or haunting the paperback stand at the hotel, where the collection ran mainly to romances and specialty items, like *The World's Best Dirty Jokes*, a volume in which all the jokes seemed to begin: "A midget went into a whorehouse . . ."

In fact the only news I wanted from outside increasingly turned out to be that which had originated in El Salvador: all other information seemed beside the point, the point being here, now, the situation, the *problema*, what did they mean the Hughes 500-D was *comprado en Guatemala*, was the Río Seco passable, were there or were there not American advisers on patrol in Usulután, who was going out, where were the roadblocks, were they burning cars today. In this context the rest of the world tended to recede, and word from the United States seemed profoundly remote, even inexplicable. I recall one morning picking up this message, from my secretary in Los Angeles: "JDD: Alessandra Stanley from *Time*, 213/273-1530. They heard you were in El Salvador and wanted some input from you for the cover story they're preparing on the women's movement. Ms. Stanley wanted their correspondent in Central America to contact you—I said that you could not be reached but would be calling me. She wanted you to call: Jay Cocks 212/841-2633." I studied this message for a long time, and tried to imagine the scenario in which a *Time* stringer in El Salvador received, by Telex from Jay Cocks in New York, a request to do an interview on the women's movement with someone who happened to be at the Camino Real Hotel. This was not a scenario that played, and I realized then that El Salvador was as inconceivable to Jay Cocks in the high keep of the Time-Life Building in New York as this message was to me in El Salvador.

I was told in the summer of 1982 by both Alvaro Magaña and Guillermo Ungo that although each of course knew the other they were of "different generations." Magaña was fifty-six. Ungo was fifty-one. Five years is a generation in El Salvador, it being a place in which not only the rest of the world but time itself tends to contract to the here and now. History is *la matanza*, and then current events, which recede even as they happen: General José Guillermo García was in the summer of 1982 widely perceived as a fixture of long standing, an immovable object through several governments and shifts in the national temperament, a survivor. In context he was a survivor, but the context was just three years, since the Majano coup. All events earlier than the Majano coup had by then vanished into uncertain memory, and the coup itself, which took place on October 15 1979, was seen as so distant that there was common talk of the next *juventud militar*, of the cyclical readiness for rebellion of what was always referred to as "the new generation" of young officers. "We think in five-year horizons," the economic officer at the American embassy told me one day. "Anything beyond that is evolution." He was talking about not having what he called "the luxury of the long view," but there is a real sense in which the five-year horizons of the American embassy constitute the longest view taken in El Salvador, either forward or back.

One reason no one looks back is that the view could only dispirit: this is a national history peculiarly resistant to heroic interpretation. There is no *libertador* to particularly remember. Public statues in San Salvador tend toward representations of abstracts, the Winged Liberty downtown, the *Salvador del Mundo* at the junction of Avenida Roosevelt and Paseo Escalón and the Santa Tecla highway; the expressionist spirit straining upward, outsized hands thrust toward the sky, at the Monument of the Revolution up by the Hotel Presidente. If the country's history as a republic seems devoid of shared purpose or unifying event, a record of insensate ambitions and their accidental consequences, its three centuries as a colony seem blanker still: Spanish colonial life was centered in Colombia and Panama to the south and Guatemala to the north, and Salvador lay between, a neglected frontier of the Captaincy General of Guatemala from 1525 until 1821, the year Guatemala declared its independence from Spain. So attenuated was El Salvador's sense of itself in its moment of independence that it petitioned the United States for admission to the union as a state. The United States declined.

In fact El Salvador had always been a frontier, even before the Spaniards arrived. The great Mesoamerican cultures penetrated this far south only shallowly. The great South American cultures thrust this far north only sporadically. There is a sense in which the place remains marked by the meanness and discontinuity of all frontier history, by a certain frontier proximity to the cultural zero. Some aspects of the local culture were imposed. Others were borrowed. An instructive moment: at an exhibition of native crafts in Nahuizalco, near Sonsonate, it was explained to me that a traditional native craft was the making of wicker furniture, but that little of this furniture was now seen because it was hard to obtain wicker in the traditional way. I asked what the traditional way of obtaining wicker had been. The traditional way of obtaining wicker, it turned out, had been to import it from Guatemala.

In fact there were a number of instructive elements about this day I spent in Nahuizalco, a hot Sunday in June. The event for which I had driven down from San Salvador was not merely a craft exhibit but the opening of a festival that would last several days, the sixth annual Feria Artesanal de Nahuizalco, sponsored by the Casa de la Cultura program of the Ministry of Education as part of its effort to encourage indigenous culture. Since public policy in El Salvador has veered unerringly toward the elimination of the indigenous population, this official celebration of its culture seemed an undertaking of some ambiguity, particularly in Nahuizalco: the uprising that led to the 1932 *matanza* began and ended among the Indian workers on the coffee *fincas* in this part of the country, and Nahuizalco and the other Indian villages around Sonsonate lost an entire generation to the *matanza*. By the early sixties estimates of the remaining Indian population in all of El Salvador ranged only between four and sixteen percent; the rest of the population was classified as *ladino*, a cultural rather than an ethnic designation, denoting only Hispanization, including both acculturated Indians and *mestizos*, and rejected by those upper-class members of the population who preferred to emphasize their Spanish ancestry.

Nineteen thirty-two was a year around Nahuizalco when Indians were tied by their thumbs and shot against church walls, shot on the road and left for the dogs, shot and bayoneted into the mass graves they themselves had dug. Indian dress was abandoned by the survivors. Nahuatl, the Indian language, was no longer spoken in public. In many ways race remains the ineffable element at the heart of this particular darkness: even as he conducted the *matanza*, General Maximiliano Hernández Martínez was dismissed, by many of the very oligarchs whose interests he was protecting by killing Indians, as "the little Indian." On this hot Sunday fifty years later the celebrants of Nahuizalco's indigenous culture would arrange themselves, by noon, into two distinct camps, the *ladinos* sitting in the shade of the schoolyard, the Indians squatting in the brutal sun outside. In the schoolyard there were trees, and tables, where the Queen of the Fair, who had a wicker crown and European features, sat with the local *guardia*, each of whom had an automatic weapon, a sidearm, and a bayonet. The *guardia* drank beer and played with their weapons. The Queen of the Fair studied her oxblood-red fingernails. It took twenty centavos to enter the schoolyard, and a certain cultural confidence.

There had been Indian dances that morning. There had been music. There had been the "blessing of the market": the statue of San Juan Bautista carried, on a platform trimmed with wilted gladioli, from the church to the market, the school, the homes of the bed-ridden. To the extent that Catholic mythology has been over four centuries successfully incorporated into local Indian life, this blessing of the market was at least part of the "actual" indigenous culture, but the dances and the music derived from other traditions. There was a Suprema Beer sound truck parked in front of the Casa de la Cultura office on the plaza, and the music that blared all day from its loudspeakers was "Roll Out the Barrel," "La Cucaracha," "Everybody Salsa."

The provenance of the dances was more compli-cated. They were Indian, but they were less remem-bered than recreated, and as such derived not from local culture but from a learned idea of local culture, an official imposition made particularly ugly by the cultural impotence of the participants. The women, awkward and uncomfortable in an approximation of native costume, moved with difficulty into the dusty street and performed a listless and unpracticed dance with baskets. Whatever men could be found (mainly little boys and old men, since those young men still alive in places like Nahuizalco try not to be noticed) had been dressed in "warrior" costume: headdresses of crinkled foil, swords of cardboard and wood. Their hair was lank, their walk furtive. Some of them wore sunglasses. The others averted their eyes. Their role in the fair involved stamping and lunging and brandishing their cardboard weapons, a display of warrior *machismo*, and the extent to which each of them had been unmanned—unmanned not only by history but by a factor less abstract, unmanned by the real weapons in the schoolyard, by the G-3 assault rifles with which the *guardia* played while they drank beer with the Queen of the Fair—rendered this display deeply obscene.

I had begun before long to despise the day, the dirt, the blazing sun, the pervasive smell of rotting meat, the absence of even the most rudimentary skill in the handicrafts on exhibit (there were sewn items, for example, but they were sewn by machine of sleazy fabric, and the simplest seams were crooked), the brutalizing music from the sound truck, the tedium; had begun most of all to despise the fair itself, which seemed contrived, pernicious, a kind of official opiate, an attempt to recreate or perpetuate a way of life neither economically nor socially viable. There was no pleasure in this day. There was a great deal of joyless milling. There was some shade in the plaza, from trees plastered with ARENA posters, but nowhere to sit. There was a fountain painted bright blue inside, but the dirty water was surrounded by barbed wire, and the sign read: "Se Prohibe Sentarse Aqui," no sitting allowed.

I stood for a while and watched the fountain. I bought a John Deere cap for seven *colones* and stood in the sun and watched the little ferris wheel, and the merry-go-round, but there seemed to be no children with the money or will to ride them, and after a while I crossed the plaza and went into the church, avoiding the bits of masonry which still fell from the bell tower damaged that week in the earthquake and its after-shocks. In the church a mass baptism was taking place: thirty or forty infants and older babies, and probably a few hundred mothers and grandmothers and aunts and godmothers. The altar was decorated with asters in condensed milk cans. The babies fretted, and several of the mothers produced bags of Fritos to quiet them. A piece of falling masonry bounced off a scaffold in the back of the church, but no one looked back. In this church full of women and babies there were only four men present. The reason for this may have been cultural, or may have had to do with the time and the place, and the G-3s in the schoolyard.

During the week before I flew down to El Salvador a Salvadoran woman who works for my husband and me in Los Angeles gave me repeated instructions about what we must and must not do. We must not go out at night. We must stay off the street whenever possible. We must never ride in buses or taxis, never leave the capital, never imagine that our passports would protect us. We must not even consider the hotel a safe place: people were killed in hotels. She spoke with considerable vehemence, because two of her brothers had been killed in Salvador in August of 1981, in their beds. The throats of both brothers had been slashed. Her father had been cut but stayed alive. Her mother had been beaten. Twelve of her other relatives, aunts and uncles and cousins, had been taken from their houses one night the same August, and their bodies had been found some time later, in a ditch. I assured her that we would remember, we would be careful, we would in fact be so careful that we would probably (trying for a light touch) spend all our time in church.

She became still more agitated, and I realized that I had spoken as a *norteamericana:* churches had not been to this woman the neutral ground they had been to me. I must remember: Archbishop Romero killed saying mass in the chapel of the Divine Providence Hospital in San Salvador. I must remember: more than thirty people killed at Archbishop Romero's funeral in the Metropolitan Cathedral in San Salvador. I must remember: more than twenty people killed before that on the steps of the Metropolitan Cathedral. CBS had filmed it. It had been on television, the bodies jerking, those still alive crawling over the dead as they tried to get out of range. I must understand: the Church was dangerous.

I told her that I understood, that I knew all that, and I did, abstractly, but the specific meaning of the Church she knew eluded me until I was actually there, at the Metropolitan Cathedral in San Salvador, one afternoon when rain sluiced down its corrugated plastic windows and puddled around the supports of the Sony and Phillips billboards near the steps. The effect of the Metropolitan Cathedral is immediate, and entirely literary. This is the cathedral that the late Archbishop Oscar Arnulfo Romero refused to finish, on the premise that the work of the Church took precedence over its display, and the high walls of raw concrete bristle with structural rods, rusting now, staining the concrete, sticking out at wrenched and violent angles. The wiring is exposed. Fluorescent tubes hang askew. The great high altar is backed by warped plyboard. The cross on the altar is of bare incandescent bulbs, but the bulbs, that afternoon, were unlit: there was in fact no light at all on the main altar, no light on the cross, no light on the globe of the world that showed the northern American continent in gray and the southern in white; no light on the dove above the globe, *Salvador del Mundo*. In this vast brutalist space that was the cathedral, the unlit altar seemed to offer a single ineluctable message: at this time and in this place the light of the world could be construed as out, off, extinguished.

In many ways the Metropolitan Cathedral is an authentic piece of political art, a statement for El Salvador as *Guernica* was for Spain. It is quite devoid of sentimental relief. There are no decorative or architectural references to familiar parables, in fact no stories at all, not even the Stations of the Cross. On the afternoon I was there the flowers laid on the altar were dead. There were no traces of normal parish activity. The doors were open to the barricaded main steps, and down the steps there was a spill of red paint, lest anyone forget the blood shed there. Here and there on the cheap linoleum inside the cathedral there was what seemed to be actual blood, dried in spots, the kind of spots dropped by a slow hemorrhage, or by a woman who does not know or does not care that she is menstruating.

There were several women in the cathedral during the hour or so I spent there, a young woman with a baby, an older woman in house slippers, a few others, all in black. One of the women walked the aisles as if by compulsion, up and down, across and back, crooning loudly as she walked. Another knelt without moving at the tomb of Archbishop Romero in the right transept. "LOOR A MONSENOR ROMERO," the crude needlepoint tapestry by the tomb read, "Praise to Monsignor Romero from the Mothers of the Imprisoned, the Disappeared, and the Murdered," the *Comité de Madres y Familiares de Presos, Desaparecidos, y Asesinados Politicos de El Salvador.*

The tomb itself was covered with offerings and petitions, notes decorated with motifs cut from greeting cards and cartoons. I recall one with figures cut from a Bugs Bunny strip, and another with a pencil drawing of a baby in a crib. The baby in this drawing seemed to be receiving medication or fluid or blood intravenously, through the IV line shown on its wrist. I studied the notes for a while and then went back and looked again at the unlit altar, and at the red paint on the main steps, from which it was possible to see the guardsmen on the balcony of the National Palace hunching back to avoid the rain. Many Salvadorans are offended by the Metropolitan Cathedral, which is as it should be, because the place remains perhaps the only unambiguous political statement in El Salvador, a metaphorical bomb in the ultimate power station.

". . . I had nothing more to do in San Salvador. I had given a lecture on the topic that had occurred to me on the train to Tapachula: Little-known Books by Famous American Authors—*Pudd'nhead Wilson*, *The Devil's Dictionary*, *The Wild Palms*. I had looked at the university; and no one could explain why there was a mural of Marx, Engels, and Lenin in the university of this right-wing dictatorship."

—Paul Theroux, *The Old Patagonian Express*.

The university Paul Theroux visited in San Salvador was the National University of El Salvador. This visit (and, given the context, this extraordinary lecture) took place in the late seventies, a period when the National University was actually open. In 1972 the Molina government had closed it, forcibly, with tanks and artillery and planes, and had kept it closed until 1974. In 1980 the Duarte government again moved troops onto the campus, which then had an enrollment of about 30,000, leaving fifty dead and offices and laboratories systematically smashed. By the time I visited El Salvador a few classes were being held in storefronts around San Salvador, but no one other than an occasional reporter had been allowed to enter the campus since the day the troops came in. Those reporters allowed to look had described walls still splashed with the spray-painted slogans left by the students, floors littered with tangled computer tape and with copies of what the National Guardsmen in charge characterized as *subversivo* pamphlets, for example a reprint of an article on inherited enzyme deficiency from *The New England Journal of Medicine.*

In some ways the closing of the National University seemed another of those Salvadoran situations in which no one came out well, and everyone was made to bleed a little, not excluding the National Guardsmen left behind to have their ignorance exposed by *gringo* reporters. The Jesuit university, UCA, or La Universidad Centroamericana José Simeón Cañas, had emerged as the most important intellectual force in the country, but the Jesuits had been so widely identified with the left that some local scholars would not attend lectures or seminars held on the UCA campus. (Those Jesuits still in El Salvador had in fact been under a categorical threat of death from the White Warriors Union since 1977. The Carter administration forced President Romero to protect the Jesuits, and on the day the killing was to have begun, July 22, 1977, the National Police are said to have sat outside the Jesuit residence in San Salvador on their motorcycles, with UZIs.) In any case UCA could manage an enrollment of only about 5,000. The scientific disciplines, which never had a particularly tenacious hold locally, had largely vanished from local life.

Meanwhile many people spoke of the National University in the present tense, as if it still existed, or as if its closing were a routine event on some long-term academic calendar. I recall talking one day to a former member of the faculty at the National University, a woman who had not seen her office since the morning she noticed the troops massing outside and left it. She lost her books and her research and the uncompleted manuscript of the book she was then writing, but she described this serenely, and seemed to find no immediate contradiction in losing her work to the Ministry of Defense and the work she did later with the Ministry of Education. The campus of the National University is said to be growing over, which is one way contradictions get erased in the tropics.

I was invited one morning to a gathering of Salvadoran writers, a kind of informal coffee hour arranged by the American embassy. For some days there had been a question about where to hold this *café literario*, since there seemed to be no single location that was not considered off-limits by at least one of the guests, and at one point the ambassador's residence was put forth as the most neutral setting. On the day before the event it was finally decided that UCA was the more appropriate place ("and just never mind," as one of the embassy people put it, that some people would not go to UCA), and at ten the next morning we gathered there in a large conference room and drank coffee and talked, at first in platitudes, and then more urgently.

These are some of the sentences spoken to me that morning: *It's not possible to speak of intellectual life in El Salvador. Every day we lose more. We are regressing constantly. Intellectual life is drying up. You are looking at the intellectual life of El Salvador. Here. In this room. We are the only survivors. Some of the others are out of the country, others are not writing because they are engaged in political activity. Some have been disappeared, many of the teachers have been dis-*

appeared. Teaching is very dangerous, if a student mis-interprets what a teacher says, then the teacher may be arrested. Some are in exile, the rest are dead. Los muer-tos, you know? We are the only ones left. There is no one after us, no young ones. It is all over, you know? At noon there was an exchange of books and *curricula vitae.* The cultural attaché from the embassy said that she, for one, would like to see this *café literario* close on a hopeful note, and someone provided one: it was a hopeful note that *norteamericanos* and *centroameri-canos* could have such a meeting. This is what passed for a hopeful note in San Salvador in the summer of 1982.

THE Ambassador of the United States of America in El Salvador, Deane Hinton, received on his desk every morning in the summer of 1982 a list of the American military personnel in-country that day. The number on this list, I was told, was never to exceed 55. Some days there were as few as 35. If the number got up to 55, and it was thought essential to bring in someone else, then a trade was made: the incoming American was juggled against an outgoing American, one normally stationed in Salvador but shunted down to Panama for as long as necessary to maintain the magic number.

Everything to do with the United States Military Group, or MILGP, was treated by the embassy as a kind of magic, a totemic presence circumscribed by potent taboos. The American A-37Bs presented to El Salvador in June of that year were actually flown up from Panama not by Americans but by Salvadorans trained at the United States Southern Air Command in Panama for this express purpose. American advisers could participate in patrols for training purposes but could not participate in patrols in combat situations. When both CBS and *The New York Times*, one day that June, reported having seen two or three American advisers in what the reporters construed as a combat situation in Usulután province, Colonel John D. Waghelstein, the MILGP commander, was called back from playing tennis in Panama (his wife had met him in Panama, there being no dependents allowed in El Salvador) in order, as he put it, "to deal with the press."

I happened to arrive for lunch at the ambassador's residence just as Colonel Waghelstein reported in from Panama that day, and the two of them, along with the embassy public affairs officer, walked to the far end of the swimming pool to discuss the day's problem out of my hearing. Colonel Waghelstein is massively built, crew-cut, tight-lipped, and very tanned, almost a cartoon of the American military presence, and the notion that he had come up from Panama to deal with the press was novel and interesting, in that he had made, during his tour in El Salvador, a pretty terse point of not dealing with the press. Some months later in Los Angeles I saw an NBC documentary in which I noticed the special effort Colonel Waghelstein had made in this case. American advisers had actually been made available to NBC, which in turn adopted a chiding tone toward CBS for the June "advisers in action" story. The total effect was mixed, however, since even as the advisers complained on camera about how "very few people" asked them what they did and about how some reporters "spend all their time with the other side," the camera angles seemed such that no adviser's face was distinctly seen. There were other points in this NBC documentary when I thought I recognized a certain official hand, for example the mention of the "sometimes cruel customs" of the Pipil Indians in El Salvador. The custom in question was that of flaying one another alive, a piece of pre-Columbian lore often tendered by embassy people as evidence that from a human-rights point of view, the trend locally is up, or at any rate holding.

Colonel Waghelstein stayed at the ambassador's that day only long enough for a drink (a Bloody Mary, which he nursed morosely), and, after he left, the ambassador and the public affairs officer and my husband and I sat down to lunch on the covered terrace. We watched a lime-throated bird in the garden. We watched the ambassador's English sheep dog bound across the lawn at the sound of shots, rifle practice at the Escuela Militar beyond the wall and down the hill. "Only time we had any quiet up here," the ambassador said in his high Montana twang, "was when we sent the whole school up to Benning." The shots rang out again. The sheep dog barked. "*Quieto*," the houseman crooned.

I have thought since about this lunch a great deal. The wine was chilled and poured into crystal glasses. The fish was served on porcelain plates that bore the American eagle. The sheep dog and the crystal and the American eagle together had on me a certain anesthetic effect, temporarily deadening that receptivity to the sinister that afflicts everyone in Salvador, and I experienced for a moment the official American delusion, the illusion of plausibility, the sense that the American undertaking in El Salvador might turn out to be, from the right angle, in the right light, just another difficult but possible mission in another troubled but possible country.

Deane Hinton is an interesting man. Before he replaced Robert White in San Salvador he had served in Europe, South America, and Africa. He had been married twice, once to an American, who bore him five children before their divorce, and once to a Chilean, who had died not long before, leaving him the stepfather of her five children by an earlier marriage. At the time I met him he had just announced his engagement to a Salvadoran named Patricia de Lopez. Someone who is about to marry a third time, who thinks of himself as the father of ten, and who has spent much of his career in chancey posts—Mombasa, Kinshasa, Santiago, San Salvador—is apt to be someone who believes in the possible.

His predecessor, Robert White, was relieved of the San Salvador embassy in February 1981, in what White later characterized as a purge, by the new Reagan people, of the State Department's entire Latin American section. This circumstance made Deane Hinton seem, to many in the United States, the bearer of the administration's big stick in El Salvador, but what Deane Hinton actually said about El Salvador differed from what Robert White said about El Salvador more in style than in substance. Deane Hinton believed, as Robert White believed, that the situation in El Salvador was bad, terrible, squalid beyond anyone's power to understand it without experiencing it. Deane Hinton also believed, as Robert White believed to a point, that the situation would be, in the absence of one or another American effort, still worse.

Deane Hinton believes in doing what he can. He had gotten arrests on the deaths of the four American churchwomen. He had even ("by yelling some more," he said) gotten the government to announce these arrests, no small accomplishment, since El Salvador was a country in which the "announcement" of an arrest did not necessarily follow the arrest itself. In the case of the murders of Michael Hammer and Mark Pearlman and José Rodolfo Viera at the Sheraton, for example, it was not the government but the American embassy which announced at least two of the various successive arrests, those of the former guardsmen Abel Campos and Rodolfo Orellana Osorio. This embassy "announcement" was reported by the American press on September 15 1982, and was followed immediately by another announcement: on September 16 1982, "a police spokesman" in San Salvador announced not the arrest but the "release" of the same suspects, after what was described as a month in custody.

To persist in so distinctly fluid a situation required a personality of considerable resistance. Deane Hinton was even then working on getting new arrests in the Sheraton murders. He was even then working on getting trials in the murders of the four American women, a trial being another step that did not, in El Salvador, necessarily follow an arrest. There had been progress. There had been the election, a potent symbol for many Americans and perhaps even for some Salvadorans, although the symbolic content of the event showed up rather better in translation than on the scene. "There was some shooting in the morning," I recall being told by a parish priest about election day in his district, "but it quieted down around nine A.M. The army had a truck going around to go out and vote—*Tu Voto Es La Solución*, you know—so they went out and voted. They wanted that stamp on their identity cards to show they voted. The stamp was the proof of their good will. Whether or not they actually wanted to vote is hard to say. I guess you'd have to say they were more scared of the army than of the guerrillas, so they voted."

Four months after the fact, in *The New York Times Magazine*, former ambassador Robert White wrote about the election: "Nothing is more symbolic of our current predicament in El Salvador than the Administration's bizarre attempt to recast D'Aubuisson in a more favorable light." Even the fact that the election had resulted in what White called "political disaster" could be presented, with a turn of the mirror, positively: one man's political disaster could be another's democratic turbulence, the birth pangs of what Assistant Secretary of State Thomas Enders persisted in calling "nascent democratic institutions." "The new Salvadoran democracy," Enders was saying five months after the election, not long after Justice of the Peace Gonzalo Alonso García, the twentieth prominent Christian Democrat to be kidnapped or killed since the election, had been dragged from his house in San Cayetano Itepeque by fifteen armed men, "is doing what it is supposed to do—bringing a broad spectrum of forces and factions into a functioning democratic system."

In other words even the determination to eradicate the opposition could be interpreted as evidence that the model worked. There was still, moreover, a certain obeisance to the land reform program, the lustrous intricacies of which were understood by so few that almost any interpretation could be construed as possible. "About 207, 207 always applied only to 1979, that is what no one understands," I had been told by President Magaña when I tried at one point to get straight the actual status of Decree 207, the legislation meant to implement the "Land-to-the-Tiller" program by providing that title to all land farmed by tenants be transferred immediately to those tenants. "There is no one more conservative than a small farmer," Peter Shiras, a former consultant to the Inter-American Development Bank, had quoted an AID official as saying about 207. "We're going to be breeding capitalists like rabbits."

Decree 207 had been the source of considerable confusion and infighting during the weeks preceding my arrival in El Salvador, suspended but not suspended, on and off and on again, but I had not before heard anyone describe it, as President Magaña seemed to be describing it, as a proposition wound up to self-destruct. Did he mean, I asked carefully, that Decree 207, implementing Land-to-the-Tiller, applied only to 1979 because no landowner, in practice, would work against his own interests by allowing tenants on his land after 207 took effect? "Right!" President Magaña had said, as if to a slow student. "Exactly! This is what no one understands. There were no new rental contracts in 1980 or 1981. No one would rent out land under 207, they would have to be crazy to do that."

What he said was obvious, but out of line with the rhetoric, and this conversation with President Magaña about Land-to-the-Tiller, which I had heard described through the spring as a centerpiece of United States policy in El Salvador, had been one of many occasions when the American effort in El Salvador seemed based on auto-suggestion, a dreamwork devised to obscure any intelligence that might trouble the dreamer. This impression persisted, and I was struck, a few months later, by the suggestion in the report on El Salvador released by the Permanent Select Committee on Intelligence of the House of Representatives (*U.S. Intelligence Performance in Central America: Achievements and Selected Instances of Concern*) that the intelligence was itself a dreamwork, tending to support policy, the report read, "rather than inform it," providing "reinforcement more than illumination," " 'ammunition' rather than analysis."

A certain tendency to this kind of dreamwork, to improving upon rather than illuminating the situation, may have been inevitable, since the unimproved situation in El Salvador was such that to consider it was to consider moral extinction. "This time they won't get away with it," Robert White was reported to have said as he watched the bodies of the four American women dragged from their common grave, but they did, and White was brought home. This is a country that cracks

Americans, and Deane Hinton gave the sense of a man determined not to crack. There on the terrace of the official residence on Avenida La Capilla in the San Benito district it was all logical. One step followed another, progress was slow. We were Americans, we would not be demoralized. It was not until late in the lunch, at a point between the salad and the profiteroles, that it occurred to me that we were talking exclusively about the appearances of things, about how the situation might be made to look better, about trying to get the Salvadoran government to "appear" to do what the American government needed done in order to make it "appear" that the American aid was justified.

It was sometimes necessary to stop Roberto D'Aubuisson "on the one-yard line" (Deane Hinton's phrase about the ARENA attempt to commandeer the presidency) because Roberto D'Aubuisson made a negative appearance in the United States, made things, as Jeremiah O'Leary, the assistant to national security adviser William Clark, had imagined Hinton advising D'Aubuisson after the election, "hard for everybody." What made a positive appearance in the United States, and things easier for everybody, were elections, and the announcement of arrests in cases involving murdered Americans, and ceremonies in which tractable *campesinos* were awarded land titles by army officers, and the Treasury Police sat on the platform, and the president came, by helicopter. "Our land reform program," Leonel Gómez, who had worked with the murdered José Rodolfo Viera in the Salvadoran Institute of Agrarian Transformation, noted in *Food Monitor*, "gave them an opportunity to build up points for the next U.S. AID grant." By "them" Leonel Gómez meant not his compatriots but Americans, meant the American Institute for Free Labor Development, meant Roy Prosterman, the architect of the Land-to-the-Tiller programs in both El Salvador and Vietnam.

In this light the American effort had a distinctly circular aspect (the aid was the card with which we got the Salvadorans to do it our way, and appearing to do it our way was the card with which the Salvadorans got the aid), and the question of why the effort was being made went unanswered. It was possible to talk about Cuba and Nicaragua, and by extension the Soviet Union, and national security, but this seemed only to justify a momentum already underway: no one could doubt that Cuba and Nicaragua had at various points supported the armed opposition to the Salvadoran government, but neither could anyone be surprised by this, or, given what could be known about the players, be unequivocally convinced that American interests lay on one side or another of what even Deane Hinton referred to as a civil war.

It was certainly possible to describe some members of the opposition, as Deane Hinton had, as "out-and-out Marxists," but it was equally possible to describe other members of the opposition, as the embassy had at the inception of the FDR in April of 1980, as "a broad-based coalition of moderate and center-left groups." The right in El Salvador never made this distinction: to the right, anyone in the opposition was a communist, along with most of the American press, the Catholic Church, and, as time went by, all Salvadoran citizens not of the right. In other words there remained a certain ambiguity about political terms as they were understood in the United States and in El Salvador, where "left" may mean, in the beginning, only a resistance to seeing one's family killed or disappeared. That it comes eventually to mean something else may be, to the extent that the United States has supported the increasing polarization in El Salvador, the Procrustean bed we made ourselves.

It was a situation in which American interests would seem to have been best served by attempting to isolate the "out-and-out Marxists" while supporting the "broad-based coalition of moderate and center-left groups," discouraging the one by encouraging the other, co-opting the opposition; but American policy, by accepting the invention of "communism," as defined by the right in El Salvador, as a daemonic element to be opposed at even the most draconic cost, had in fact achieved the reverse. "We believe in gringos," Hugh Barrera, an ARENA contender for the presidency, told Laurie Becklund of *The Los Angeles Times* when she asked in April of 1982 if ARENA did not fear losing American aid by trying to shut the Christian Democrats out of the government. "Congress would not risk losing a whole country over one party. That would be turning against a U.S. ally and encouraging Soviet intervention here. It would not be intelligent." In other words "anti-communism" was seen, correctly, as the bait the United States would always take.

That we had been drawn, both by a misapprehension of the local rhetoric and by the manipulation of our own rhetorical weaknesses, into a game we did not understand, a play of power in a political tropic alien to us, seemed apparent, and yet there we remained. In this light all arguments tended to trail off. Pros and cons seemed equally off the point. At the heart of the American effort there was something of the familiar ineffable, as if it were taking place not in El Salvador but in a mirage of El Salvador, the mirage of a society not unlike our own but "sick," a temporarily fevered republic in which the antibodies of democracy needed only to be encouraged, in which words had stable meanings north and south ("election," say, and "Marxist") and in which there existed, waiting to be tapped by our support, some latent good will. A few days before I arrived in El Salvador there appeared in *Diario de Hoy* a full-page advertisement placed by leaders of the Women's Crusade for Peace and Work. This advertisement accused the United States, in the person of its ambassador, Deane Hinton, of "blackmailing us with your miserable aid, which only keeps us subjugated in underdevelopment so that powerful countries like yours can continue exploiting our few riches and having us under your boot." The Women's Crusade for Peace and Work is an organization of the right, with links to ARENA, which may suggest how latent that good will remains.

This "blackmail" motif, and its arresting assumption that trying to keep Salvadorans from killing one another constituted a new and particularly crushing imperialism, began turning up more and more frequently. By October of 1982 advertisements were appearing in the San Salvador papers alleging that the blackmail was resulting in a "betrayal" of El Salvador by the military, who were seen as "lackeys" of the United States. At a San Salvador Chamber of Commerce meeting in late October, Deane Hinton said that "in the first two weeks of this month at least sixty-eight human beings were murdered in El Salvador under circumstances which are familiar to everyone here," stressed that American aid was dependent upon "progress" in this area, and fielded some fifty written questions, largely hostile, one of which read, "Are you trying to blackmail us?"

I was read this speech over the telephone by an embassy officer, who described it as "the ambassador's strongest statement yet." I was puzzled by this, since the ambassador had made most of the same points, at a somewhat lower pitch, in a speech on February 11, 1982; it was hard to discern a substantive advance between, in February, "If there is one issue which could force our Congress to withdraw or seriously reduce its support for El Salvador, it is the issue of human rights," and, in October: "If not, the United States—in spite of our other interests, in spite of our commitment to the struggle against communism, could be forced to deny assistance to El Salvador." In fact the speeches seemed almost cyclical, seasonal events keyed to the particular rhythm of the six-month certification process; midway in the certification cycle things appear "bad," and are then made, at least rhetorically, to appear "better," "improvement" being the key to certification.

I mentioned the February speech on the telephone, but the embassy officer to whom I was speaking did not see the similarity; this was, he said, a "stronger" statement, and would be "front-page" in both *The Washington Post* and *The Los Angeles Times*. In fact the story did appear on the front pages of both *The Washington Post* and *The Los Angeles Times*, suggesting that every six months the news is born anew in El Salvador.

Whenever I hear someone speak now of one or another *solución* for El Salvador I think of particular Americans who have spent time there, each in his or her own way inexorably altered by the fact of having been in a certain place at a certain time. Some of these Americans have since moved on and others remain in Salvador, but, like survivors of a common natural disaster, they are equally marked by the place.

"There are a lot of options that aren't playable. We could come in militarily and shape the place up. That's an option, but it's not playable, because of public opinion. If it weren't for public opinion, however, El Salvador would be the ideal laboratory for a full-scale military operation. It's small. It's self-contained. There are hemispheric cultural similarities."

—*A United States embassy officer in San Salvador.*

"June 15th was not only a great day for El Salvador, receiving $5 million in additional U.S. aid for the private sector and a fleet of fighter planes and their corresponding observation units, but also a great day for me. Ray Bonner [of *The New York Times*] actually spoke to me at Ilopango airport and took my hand and shook it when I offered it to him. . . . Also, another correspondent pulled me aside and said that if I was such a punctilious journalist why the hell had I written something about him that wasn't true. Here I made no attempt to defend myself but only quoted my source. Later we talked and ironed out some wrinkles. It is a great day when journalists with opposing points of view can get together and learn something from each other, after all, we are all on the same side. I even wrote a note to Robert E. White (which he ignored) not long ago after he protested that I had not published his Letter to the Editor (which I had) suggesting that we be friendly enemies. The only enemy is totalitarianism, in any guise: communistic, socialistic, capitalistic or militaristic. Man is unique because he has free will and the capacity to choose. When this is suppressed he is no longer a man but an animal. That is why I say that despite differing points of view, we are none of us enemies."

—*Mario Rosenthal, editor of the* El Salvador News Gazette, *in his June 14–20 1982 column, "A Great Day."*

"You would have had the last interview with an obscure Salvadoran."

—*An American reporter to whom I had mentioned that I had been trying to see Colonel Salvador Beltrán Luna on the day he died in a helicopter crash.*

"It's not as bad as it could be. I was talking to the political risk people at one of the New York banks and in 1980 they gave El Salvador only a ten percent chance of as much stability in 1982 as we have now. So you see."

—*The same embassy officer.*

"Normally I wouldn't have a guard at my level, but there were death threats against my predecessor, he was on a list. I'm living in his old house. In fact something kind of peculiar happened today. Someone telephoned and wanted to know, very urgent, how to reach the Salvadoran woman with whom my predecessor lived. This person on the phone claimed that the woman's family needed to reach her, a death, or illness, and she had left no

100

address. This might have been true and it might not have been true. Naturally I gave no information."

—Another embassy officer.

"AMBASSADOR WHITE: My embassy also sent in several months earlier these captured documents. There is no doubt about the provenance of these documents as they were handed to me directly by Colonel Adolfo Majano, then a member of the junta. They were taken when they captured ex-Major D'Aubuisson and a number of other officers who were conspiring against the Government of El Salvador.

SENATOR ZORINSKY: . . . Please continue, Mr. Ambassador.

AMBASSADOR WHITE: I would be glad to give you copies of these documents for your record. In these documents there are over a hundred names of people who are participating, both within the Salvadoran military as active conspirers against the Government, and also the names of people living in the United States and in Guatemala City who are actively funding the death squads. I gave this document, in Spanish, to three of the most skilled political analysts I know in El Salvador without orienting them in any way. I just asked them to read this and tell me what conclusions they came up with. All three of them came up with the conclusion that there is, within this document, evidence that is compelling, if not 100 percent conclusive, that D'Aubuisson and his group are responsible for the murder of Archbishop Romero. SENATOR CRANSTON: What did you say? Responsible for whose murder? AMBASSADOR WHITE: Archbishop Romero . . ."

—From the record of hearings before the Committee on Foreign Relations, U.S. Senate, April 9, 1981, two months after Robert White left San Salvador.

Of all these Americans I suppose I think especially of Robert White, for his is the authentic American voice afflicted by El Salvador: *You will find one of the pages with Monday underlined and with quotation marks,* he said that April day in 1981 about his documents, which were duly admitted into the record and, as the report of the House Permanent Select Committee on Intelligence later concluded, ignored by the CIA; he talked about Operation Pineapple, and blood sugar, and 257 Roberts guns, about addresses in Miami, about Starlight scopes; about *documents handed to him directly by Colonel Majano,* about *compelling if not conclusive evidence* of activities that continued to fall upon the ears of his auditors as signals from space, unthinkable, inconceivable, dim impulses from a black hole. In the serene light of Washington that spring day in 1981, two months out of San Salvador, Robert White's distance from the place was already lengthening: in San Salvador he might have wondered, the final turn of the mirror, *what Colonel Majano had to gain by handing him the documents.*

That the texture of life in such a situation is essentially untranslatable became clear to me only recently, when I tried to describe to a friend in Los Angeles an incident that occurred some days before I left El Salvador. I had gone with my husband and another American to the San Salvador morgue, which, unlike most morgues in the United States, is easily accessible, through an open door on the ground floor around the back of the court building. We had been too late that morning to see the day's bodies (there is not much emphasis on embalming in El Salvador, or for that matter on identification, and bodies are dispatched fast for disposal), but the man in charge had opened his log to show us the morning's entries, seven bodies, all male, none identified, none believed older than twenty-five. Six had been certified dead by *arma de fuego*, firearms, and the seventh, who had also been shot, of shock. The slab on which the bodies had been received had already been washed down, and water stood on the floor. There were many flies, and an electric fan.

The other American with whom my husband and I had gone to the morgue that morning was a newspaper reporter, and since only seven unidentified bodies bearing evidence of *arma de fuego* did not in San Salvador in the summer of 1982 constitute a newspaper story worth pursuing, we left. Outside in the parking lot there were a number of wrecked or impounded cars, many of them shot up, upholstery chewed by bullets, windshield shattered, thick pastes of congealed blood on pearlized hoods, but this was also unremarkable, and it was not until we walked back around the building to the reporter's rented car that each of us began to sense the potentially remarkable.

Surrounding the car were three men in uniform, two on the sidewalk and the third, who was very young, sitting on his motorcycle in such a way as to block our leaving. A second motorcycle had been pulled up directly behind the car, and the space in front was occupied. The three had been joking among themselves, but the laughter stopped as we got into the car. The reporter turned the ignition on, and waited. No one moved. The two men on the sidewalk did not meet our eyes. The boy on the motorcycle stared directly, and caressed the G-3 propped between his thighs. The reporter asked in Spanish if one of the motorcycles could be moved so that we could get out. The men on the sidewalk said nothing, but smiled enigmatically. The boy only continued staring, and began twirling the flash suppressor on the barrel of his G-3.

This was a kind of impasse. It seemed clear that if we tried to leave and scraped either motorcycle the situation would deteriorate. It also seemed clear that if we did not try to leave the situation would deteriorate. I studied my hands. The reporter gunned the motor, forced the car up onto the curb far enough to provide a minimum space in which to maneuver, and managed to back out clean. Nothing more happened, and what did happen had been a common enough kind of incident in El Salvador, a pointless confrontation with aimless authority, but I have heard of no *solución* that precisely addresses this local vocation for terror.

Any situation can turn to terror. The most ordinary errand can go bad. Among Americans in El Salvador there is an endemic apprehension of danger in the apparently benign. I recall being told by a network anchor man that one night in his hotel room (it was at the time of the election, and because the Camino Real was full he had been put up at the Sheraton) he took the mattress off the bed and shoved it against the window. He happened to have with him several bullet-proof vests that he had brought from New York for the camera crew, and before going to the Sheraton lobby he put one on. Managers of American companies in El Salvador (Texas Instruments is still there, and Cargill, and some others) are replaced every several months, and their presence is kept secret. Some companies bury their managers in a number-two or number-three post. American embassy officers are driven in armored and unmarked vans (no eagle, no seal, no CD plates) by Salvadoran drivers and Salvadoran guards, because, I was told, "if someone gets blown away, obviously the State Department would prefer it done by a local security man, then you don't get headlines saying 'American Shoots Salvadoran Citizen.'" These local security men carry automatic weapons on their laps.

In such a climate the fact of being in El Salvador comes to seem a sentence of indeterminate length, and the prospect of leaving doubtful. On the night before I was due to leave I did not sleep, lay awake and listened to the music drifting up from a party at the Camino Real pool, heard the band play "Malaguena" at three and at four and again at five A.M., when the party seemed to end and light broke and I could get up. I was picked up to go to the airport that morning by one of the embassy vans, and a few blocks from the hotel I was seized by the conviction that this was not the most direct way to the airport, that this was not an embassy guard sitting in front with the Remington on his lap; that this was someone else. That the van turned out in fact to be the embassy van, detouring into San Benito to pick up an AID official, failed to relax me: once at the airport I sat without moving and averted my eyes from the soldiers patrolling the empty departure lounges.

When the nine A.M. TACA flight to Miami was announced I boarded without looking back, and sat rigid until the plane left the ground. I did not fasten my seat belt. I did not lean back. The plane stopped that morning at Belize, setting down on the runway lined with abandoned pillboxes and rusting camouflaged tanks to pick up what seemed to be every floater on two continents, wildcatters, collectors of information, the fantasts of the hemisphere. Even a team of student missionaries got on at Belize, sallow children from the piney woods of Georgia and Alabama who had been teaching the people of Belize, as the team member who settled down next to me explained, to know Jesus as their personal savior.

He was perhaps twenty, with three hundred years of American hill stock in his features, and as soon as the plane left Belize he began filling out a questionnaire on his experience there, laboriously printing out the phrases, *in obedience to God, opportunity to renew commitment, most rewarding part of my experience, most disheartening part.* Somewhere over the Keys I asked him what the most disheartening part of his experience had been. The most disheartening part of his experience, he said, had been seeing people leave the Crusade as empty as they came. The most rewarding part of his experience had been renewing his commitment to bring the Good News of Jesus as personal savior to all these different places. The different places to which he was committed to bring the Good News were New Zealand, Iceland, Finland, Colorado, and El Salvador. This was *la solución* not from Washington or Panama or Mexico but from Belize, and the piney woods of Georgia. This flight from San Salvador to Belize to Miami took place at the end of June 1982. In the week that I am completing this report, at the end of October 1982, the offices in the Hotel Camino Real in San Salvador of the Associated Press, United Press International, United Press International Television News, NBC News, CBS News, and ABC News were raided and searched by members of the El Salvador National Police carrying submachine guns; fifteen leaders of legally recognized political and labor groups opposing the government of El Salvador were disappeared in San Salvador; Deane Hinton said that he was "reasonably certain" that these disappearances had not been conducted under Salvadoran government orders; the Salvadoran Ministry of Defense announced that eight of the fifteen disappeared citizens were in fact in government custody; and the State Department announced that the Reagan administration believed that it had "turned the corner" in its campaign for political stability in Central America.